A GUIDE TO THE ALHAMBRA
AND GENERALIFE

To my father,
in the living memory of his Alhambra.

By Jesús Bermúdez López

2.ª Agosto 1999
© Editorial En su Mano. Telf. 958 22 51 77
Fotografías: M. Corral
Diseño Gráfico: F. García
Fotocomposición: Felix Amoretti
Fotomecánica: Trama color
Impreso en España
I.S.B.N.: 84-86320-12-7
Depósito Legal: M-23123-1987

INDEX

PREFACE

Almost a century of excavation work and exploration of the terrain, buildings and architectural remains of the Alhambra and its surroundings have uncovered a wealth of knowledge, perhaps based somewhat more on speculation than erudition, but which nonetheless enables us to piece together information of hitherto unknown aspects of this world-renowned monument.

One should also bear in mind that the Alhambra is visited by many thousands of tourists every year, and its beautiful gardens and scenery provide an incomparable setting for both cultural and social events which go beyond the simple function of its protection and preservation as a monument.

Circumstances, therefore, now impose the necessity for a new approach to visiting and presenting the **Alhambra,** yet at the same time not detracting from the peculiarities of this monumental complex, recognised for its artistic and historic value as long ago as the Middle Ages. Since then it has undergone continuous transformation depending on the demands and circumstances of the different moments during its very long and varied existence.

The Early Middle Ages and Renaissance were by far the two periods which most patently marked and enriched the sight we admire today. The ideal for the preservation of the Alhambra during the century of exploration and recovery work was that of saving all that was valuable or quaint from the complex succession of events in its past. Despite this, in effect there has often been an overwhelming tendency to exhalt some values to the detriment of others. Evidence from other periods was disregarded, and therefore an overpowering criterion was adopted which placed less emphasis than is due on the dualism which harmonised both the beauty and the values of the 14th and 16th centuries present within the Alhambra. Examples of this dualism are to be found in the meetings between Tendilla and Münzer or between Boscán and Navaggiero, and most especially in the nature of the Alhambra itself.

It is our aim in this **Guide to the Alhambra** to put forward new ideas and knowledge which will match the new demands of the ongoing history of a monument which has successively been used as a palace and castle, as a palatial city or garish town, as an encampment for soldiers and even gypsies, as a prison, and lastly as a paradise for poets, erudites and tourists alike.

GRANADA AND ISLAM

Both the eastern environment in which the Islamic faith was forged and the warm, dry climate of the first countries to be converted to Islam, marked a clear tendency and tradition in the arts of the Muslim populations. This overwhelmed not only an Andalusia, deeply enrooted in Romanic tradition (still very apparent today), but also the inhabitants of Granada who, even though converts to Islam, and guided by a common culture and civilization, were neither Morrocan nor Egyptian (different nations within Islam —as was al-Andalus—) but rather, Mediterranean and different.

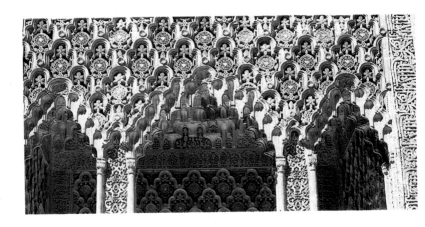

Decorative feature of the Palace of Lions.

Islamic Granada, a nation halfway between the Eastern and Western cultures, seemed exotic both to Europeans and Eastern peoples, which may be significative of its originality.

For religious and traditional, rather than monetary reasons, the Islamic architecture propagated in Granada did not consider solidity to be a noble quality. Solid walls or bare floors were enhanced with subtle architectural decoration using ceramic tiles, plaster, wood and marble contrasted with more base materials. Above all, the proportions of open space and the delightful views afforded an originality where the play of light, volume, interior and exterior spaces contrasted, yet at the same time blended and balanced harmoniously.

The decorative elements overlap one another, they contrast and interweave topics, rhythms and shapes. The plaster work, the ceramic tiles, wood and marble blocks, capitals and shafts, or even the fountains themselves forego their natural qualities when transformed to imitate cloth, metal, glass or jewels by the ornamental, aesthetic resources used.

In sharp contrast with the fortified military quarters, built to withstand sieges and attacks with the solidity of the steam chambers and furnaces for the baths designed to resist excessive dampness or heat, the remaining architectural designs are light and livian.

«Four beams and a bit of plaster and ceramics, turned into a work of art through ingenuity, sensitivity and good taste, are enough to make palaces» where their natural beauty and the artistic, symbolic antinaturalism intertwine.

In the courtyards, halls or in the gardens, water springs and flows, gurgling or murmuring, or stands still in mirror-like ponds refreshing the flower-scented air.

The open landscape invades the intimacy of the palace interiors, just as the chambers spill over into the gardened-courtyards. These are not walkways but open-air rooms, the sky their only ceiling. Imagine how relaxing and clean it would be to have a house where no fireplace smoke or cooking odours linger, although the smell of dishes prepared in an oven well away from the living quarters does drift pleasantly through the air. The cleanliness makes its presence felt in the well-equipped bathing areas. In other words, a sensitive world overlapping a world of meditation as is customary in an Eastern culture of any age or country.

Once the Islamic residences and palaces had been adapted to Christian dwellings and palaces, and later left to withstand the effects of weather and time, one hundred long years of clearing and excavation of the land and buildings were needed until it became evident that a more appropriate interpretation of the Alhambra was a priority. But the transformations which have been carried out have left us with only the coldness of a vacuum or the perfect symmetry of the prints on the walls. The **Alhambra**, nonetheless, never fails to delight, not only for its scenery and views, but because it has retained its true atmosphere and its original, authentic purpose, though now lost, is still patent today.

Thus, so many different images of the Alhambra are feasible. This explains why its name, written upon the most unlikely corners of the world, has become a synonym of fantasy. Nevertheless, it is its reality and not its invention that holds so many visitors' attention during such a brief encounter.

SUGGESTIONS

The Muslim Alhambra would be better understood if we did not attempt to perceive it through Western eyes, yet rather sought out its contrasting features. One such

The views: beautiful contrasts from the Alhambra.

example would be the contrast between the central courtyard of the Charles V Palace and the Courtyard of the Myrtles, which highlights concepts that are so intrinsically different.

Our visitor would find it useful to observe the vistas seen from lower viewpoints in the Muslim buildings; those from close to the walls or along the span of doorways and windows, capturing cross perspectives and keeping slightly away from the central axis.

The Alhambra should never be seen in haste. The visitor should have time to reflect on the numerous contrasts it has to offer. This is precisely the reason why we would recommend, if at all possible, that visitors complement our perspective of the Alhambra by reading appropriate texts, such as the very prayers and poems inscribed on the walls.

HISTORICAL BACKGROUND

Some type of citadel must have occupied the hill called he **Sabika,** where the Alhambra now stands, because of its strategical location at a vital junction and the proximity of water. Nevertheless, no mention of the so-called «**Red Castle**» is found until the year 860.

In the 11th century, Granada, for the first time in its istory, was the Muslim court for the **Zirid** dynasty, which stablished its palace and administration courtyards by the old Roman Forum, for the prestige such a location would bestow on the new government, and for its already-existing defence structure that was later to be called the **Old Alcazaba** or old citadel.

The second and last time Granada served as a Muslim court was during the reign of the **Nasrid** dynasty, responsible in the 13th century for extending the Alhambra and converting it into the seat of the sultanate —flanked by the Rivers **Darro and Genil**, with the old **Red Castle** at one extreme and the **Sierra Nevada** Mountains at the other.

The Towers of the Alhambra Palaces overlooking the Albaicin quarter.

The Nasrid dynasty reached its splendour in the 14th century, under the rule of **Yusuf I** and **Muhammad V,** at which time the most important part of the present-day **Alhambra** was built. This was about the same time as the building of the papal palace in Avignon and the grand city mansions, such as those of Bruges or Prague, York Cathedral and Westminster Abbey —more than a century before the discovery of America.

After the siege and conquest of Granada in 1492, the **Catholic Monarchs** converted the Alhambra into the **Royal Citadel** and large sums of money were spent on

9

its preservation. But due to the monarchs' desire to live there and the fact that the Royal Court was far more than the grounds could possibly accommodate, not to mention the fact that their customs were so different, a gradual transformation took place. The **Charles V** residences were later added and, since it still proved to be too small for the Emperor's European court, it was further enlarged in 1527 to include the vast Renaissance palace that stands today.

During the 18th century, preservation of the Alham

View of the Alhambra Palaces from the Generalife.

bra was seriously neglected, and although it was given some attention during the Napoleonic occupation, these efforts proved to be in vain due to the destructive withdrawal of the troops.

Soon afterwards, the Romanticists initiated the exaltation of the Alhambra, and from the reign of Elizabeth II onwards, a progressively more effective preservation of the palace began. Even before 1870, when the Alhambra was considered to be of historical and artistic value, it attracted the attention of important European literary figures who established it as a contemporary tourist focal point.

GENERAL DESCRIPTION

The Alhambra enclosure is situated, as though it were an acropolis, on the natural platform formed by the Sabika hill, running from the foothills of the Sierra Nevada mountains towards the heart of the city and its fertile valley. This barren-sloped hill, red in colour, «appeared to crown Granada like a string of rubies», which is probably the reason why it was given the name of Alhambra, meaning «The Red Hill».

The Alcazaba citadel and palatine city rose above this crown of rubies tinged with hues of flora —quinces and almond trees, lofty poplars and crab apple trees lining deep ravines, just as they have been depicted in the past century. The citadel and the palatine city were joined together, and they were also connected to the limits of the city of Granada, into which the Alhambra only partially spread, the rest remaining outside the city limits, amidst open, rough land, between valley and hillsides.

Only the **Puerta de las Armas** (the Gate of Arms), embedded at the foot of the Alcazaba, opened up along the city walls of Granada at the westernmost end of the

The Alhambra Alcazaba (Citadel) overlooking the city.

Alhambra, as the only nexus between the two urban centres.

From here, the Alhambra enclosure stretched out to the east in an irregular, elongated pattern over the hillock. Its towers conformed to the terrain and to each of their corresponding civil or military functions, which, in turn, are responsible for the great variety in size, positioning and appearance. Part of the area within the grounds is slightly raised and is referred to as the High Alhambra. Important evidence and remains have been discovered in the lower areas surrounding the High Alhambra of some seven palaces. Two of them, the Comares and Leones Palaces, were joined together after the Christian Reconquest and later enlarged during the Renaissance to form what is known today as the Royal Residence (Casa Real).

Remains have also been discovered of palatial mansions, residences for the members of the royal family, manor-houses, a mosque a madrasha, oratories, burial vaults, public and private baths, a grain exchange, market, a mint, storehouses and dungeons, and even a craftsman's quarter, in the service of the Royal Palace at the High Alhambra, and the Alcazaba military quarters.

It is most likely there were no interior bulwark walls but there were doors intercepting the alleys which divided the Alhambra up into compartments that were distributed between two main streets running almost parallel across the length of the grounds from east to west. Just inside and below the outer citadel ramparts and placed between these and the places of residence ran a parapet walk which reached around the entire grounds, sometimes passing though tunnels, under

Aerial view of the Alhambra from the east.

palaces or through the tower-palaces that loomed up over the outer wall.

On the outside to the west, lies the spur of the Alcazaba; to the north side, the steep left banks of the Darro River surrounded by the picturesque St Peter's woods.

To the east and south respectively lie the gorges cut by the natural moat that separate both the Alhambra from the Generalife along a walkway called the **Cuesta de los Chinos,** and the Alcazaba from the Vermilion Towers along another walkway called the **Cuesta de los Gomérez.** About halfway up the Cuesta de los Chinos stands the **Puerta de Hierro** (or the Gate of Iron), whose fortified walls and stables still protect the old pass to the entrance of the Generalife.

The façade of the southernmost bulwark encircling the Alhambra enclosure has two monumental gates situated at either end: the **Puerta de Siete Suelos** (or the Gate of Seven Floors), partially destroyed by bombardment during the withdrawal of the Napoleonic troops, and the gate traditionally known as the **Puerta de Justicia** (or the Gate of Justice), although the inscription on this Gate names it as the **Puerta de la Explanada** (the Esplanade Gate). It seems most likely that an esplanade did spread out before it in former days, although today's visitor will only find a wide, tree-covered gully.

The Generalife consists mainly of a palace and a number of gardens. It was perhaps the most important of the many estates the Granada sultans possessed throughout their kingdom, and is the only one with direct access to the Alhambra. It is for this reason that the Generalife, together with the Vermilion Towers and the **Campo de los Mártires** (or Field of the Martyrs) can be considered as key strategic defence points for the Alhambra.

The Generalife has undergone numerous transformations since the Christian Conquest simply because its new occupants had a style of living and customs that differed greatly from those of the Arab court. Owing to the campaign preceding the Conquest and successive periods, the Vermilion Towers must also have been greatly modified. Both enclosures, nevertheless, have preserved their original core of buildings, thus allowing us to interpret the fundamental nature of each, as well as the purpose they were intended for.

It is evident, therefore, that the Alhambra, together with its defence structure and the Generalife is the most complete medieval complex still standing in Europe. The setting itself and scenic surroundings further contribute to keeping the original spirit of the monument alive.

ITINERARY AND ACCESS TO THE ALHAMBRA

The route of a tour through the Alhambra should begin at the **Gate of Justice** for both historical and practical reasons. The most appropriate starting point in keeping with the characteristics of the Alhambra would

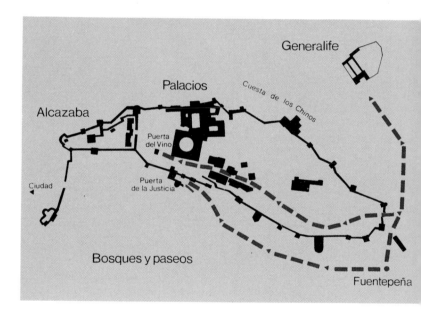

be the **Gate of Arms** since, as mentioned earlier, it was the medieval entrance from the city of Granada to the Alhambra. Today, notwithstanding, the old entrances to the Alhambra have been modified for various imperatives, although they may all be visited on a present-day tour of the Alhambra.

Those tourists coming to the Alhambra by car will find ample parking space at the **Fuentepeña** area (at the Generalife esplanade), from where they may begin their tour. There are a number of alternative routes for the sequences described in this Guide. They could first visit the **Generalife,** and then enter the Alhambra grounds by one of two routes. These two options, also available for those visitors who prefer to postpone their tour of the Generalife until the end, are as follows:

— Starting off from the **Fuentepeña** area, follow the walkway that runs down along the outside of the **Alhambra** bulwark to the south, between the **woods** and the **Paseo de las Alamedas** (Poplar Walk) as far as the **esplanade** that lies in front of the **Gate of Justice**, where the tour itself would begin. It is a slightly longer walk, but picturesque and more in keeping with the charracteristics of the Alhambra.

— Leaving from the first stretch of the **Generalife Promenade,** visitors could enter the Alhambra at the eastern end, over a recently-constructed bridge and through the ruined remains at the **High Alhambra** area, named «**Secano**» or «dry area», today the main archeological site of the Alhambra. From the 1930's on-

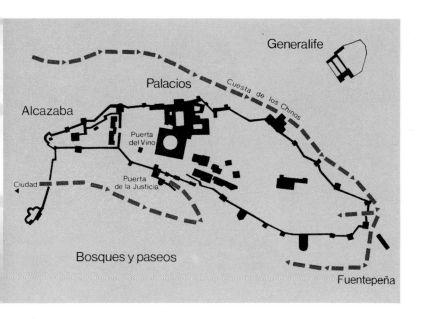

wards excavations have uncovered remains of residences, cottage industries in the service of the Alhambra Palace, and even the **Palacio de los Abencerrajes (or Palace of the Arab Courtiers)** and its recently-restored bath. At this high area of the **Medina,** or city of the Alhambra, stands one of the four entrances that used to open the city bulwark to the outside: the **Gate of the Seven Floors.** This area suffered much of the bombing during the Napoleonic withdrawal.

Another starting point would be the **Puerta del Vino,** standing at the end of a modern walkway which leads into the **Calle Real,** or Royal Avenue.

Those who choose to walk to the Alhambra via the

Cuesta de los Gomérez, through the **Puerta de las Granadas** (Gate of the Pomegranates) and up the **Alamedas** walkway to the **Pilar de Carlos V** (or Charles V Fountain), will be standing on the esplanade that stretches out in front of the **Gate of Justice,** their starting point for the tour of the Alhambra.

Pedestrians may also enter the Alhambra along a picturesque and romantic path (the **Cuesta de los Chinos**) rising from the left bank of the **Darro River** at the foot of the **Albaicín.** Running along the outer wall of the bulwark on the northeastern side of the Alhambra grounds and leaving the **Generalife** gardens behind, this walkway leads up to an area called the **Mimbre,** or Osier Bed, found next to the parking area at **Fuentepeña.**

Gate of Justice or of the Esplanade.

Finally, those arriving by public transport should likewise head towards the **Gate of Justice** as their starting point, just as should those who come up by any of the following walkways: **Cuesta de las Cremallera** or **Cuesta del Caidero,** the **Cuesta del Realejo** or the **Paseo de las Alamedas.** (These latter three are the least used by visitors to the Alhambra.)

The Wine Gate.

17

ENTRANCE TO THE ALHAMBRA

Of the four entrances found along the walled enclosure of the Alhambra, undoubtedly the most oustanding is the **Gate of Justice,** erected by **Yusuf III** in 1348. A wide horseshoe arch joins the two massive blocks that protrude from the great tower to protect the Gate's inner façade, originally very rich in colour. A commemoration of the Roman triumphal arch is inscribed immediately above the arch opening the Gate's inner entrance. An outstretched hand in the keystone of the arch at the outer entrance lies in direct alignment with a key carved in the inner arch, contrasting with the statue image of the **Virgen Mary** (work of Roberto Alemán) decreed by the Catholic Monarchs to be placed above the Arab inscription as though it were a question of talismanic signs or strange powers possessed by two very different worlds. Four embedded columns support the Gate itself, each with their respective capitals bearing inscriptions professing the Muslim faith. Between the columns, immediately inside the inner arch, the original fittings for each of the double doors

Gate of Justice and the Charles V Fountain.

(faced in iron) can still be seen. The inside of the entrance slopes up an uneven, Z-shaped passageway, a characteristic feature of this type of outer entrance gate, used for protection purposes. This inner passageway is surmounted first by an elongated groin vault, fol-

Square of the Arab Cisterns.

lowed by a cupola, then three convergent groin vaults painted in the charcteristically Nasrid style to imitate exposed red brick.

Having crossed through the Gate, turn left up a slightly sloped avenue, flanked to the left by the outer bulwark and to the right, by a series of buildings that were originally protected by a counterwall.

This avenue opens out into a expansive esplanade known as the **Plaza de los Aljibes** (or Square of the Arab Cisterns), where most tours of the Alhambra start. The routes described in this Guide can naturally be taken separately or in any sequence. We would, however, recommend visiting the **Palacio de Carlos V** (the Charles V Palace) first, followed by a visit to the **Alcazaba** (or Citadel) and later, to the **Arab Palaces.** We would also recommend a walk along the **Royal Avenue** at any point along the tour.

Following the Christian Conquest, the building of a huge Arab cistern over the natural ravine that once separated the Alcazaba from the rest of the Alhambra outbuildings gave rise to the **Square of the Arab Cisterns.**

To the immediate right, just before entering into the square, stands the fine **Wine Gate** that once served as a separation between the **Medina** or inner **Ciudadela** (fortress) of the Alhambra from the rest of the outbuildings. The Gate's outer and inner façade are said to be attributed to **Muhammad II** and **Muhammad V** respectively.

Inner façade of the Wine Gate.

The original benches where the sentries used to sit have been preserved to this day. Perpendicular to the **Wine Gate** stems the **Royal Avenue,** one of the Alhambra's two main avenues, that gradually leads up to the highest area of the enclosure at the citadel's easternmost point.

Next to the outer façade of the **Wine Gate** begins a descending walkway that once led through a number of gates (today in ruins) to the grand **Palace Esplanade,** starting point for present-day tours through the **Nasrid Palaces.**

Opposite the **Wine Gate,** at the other end of the **Square of the Arab Cisterns,** lies an impressive stretch of bulwark and towers. The itinerary for the Alcazaba tour begins at the foot of these towers.

THE ALCAZABA

Having crossed the esplanade of the **Square of the Arab Cisterns,** walk up to the military quarter of the Alhambra known as the **Alcazaba.** Access is gained through an open gate in the centre of a stretch of the 16th century bulwark mentioned above. This defence structure closes the Alcazaba off to the east and completely isolates it from the rest of the Alhambra buildings.

The Alcazaba is first surrounded by a counterwall or **barbican** which gives way to a moat of uneven width. On the northern side of this moat stands the **Gate of Arms Tower,** and the southeastern flank is overlooked by several other towers that have frequently been reconstructed throughout history.

Having entered the Alcazaba enclosure we find an impressive block of Arab bulwark, more than six metres thick, atop which rest three large towers: to the left, the **Adarguero** or Tower of the Shield Bearers, in the

The Alcazaba and Sentinel's Tower.

centre, the **Quebrada** or Broken Tower and to the right, the **Homenaje** or Homage Tower.

Heading towards the **Homage Tower,** there is a small modern stairway that leads up to the terrace of the **Torre del Cubo,** or Round Tower, so-named for its shape which does not conform to that of the other towers within the enclosure. This Tower, forming part of the outer bulwark through which access was gained to the Alcazaba, was built on by the Christians to tighten protection of the military quarters in the 16th century. A twin for the Round Tower was planned for the southern end of the bulwark, though it was never actually built. The Round Tower encased a smaller Arab one, still standing on the inside as will be seen later.

The Alcazaba Towers (the Broken, Homage, Round and Sentinel's Towers).

Throughout the tour it is worth paying special attention to the views and the contrasting play of sunlight and shadows afforded from the different towers and

balconies. The differences in height and positioning of each of the towers and the quantity of sunlight that traverses them offer multicoloured variations that further enchance the architectural profiles of the Alhambra itself, the city of Granada, the **Darro River** valley and the **Albaicín** or **Sacromonte** quarters.

In medieval fortresses, the **Homage Tower** was the most important. It was usually the tallest and best protected, since it was in this tower that the «military command post» was established and was the last to be abandoned under siege and subsequent surrender.

Turning left at the foot of the tower, the landscape opens up again at the «**Balcony of the Gypsies**» and this vantage point offers a perfect view of the superimposing stretches of bulwark that protected the Alcazaba.

Continue along the foot of the Tower, up a short V-shaped walkway, enter through a doorway in the higher bulwark structure into the Alcazaba enclosure. Close by is a postern that leads to the northern parapet walk of the citadel's barbican, used by sentries to patrol above the **Puerta de la Tahona** (Gate of the Flour Mill)

The military district.

and along the whole of the parapet surrounding the Alhambra.

The wide interior spaces inside medieval castles were usually given the name of **Courtyard of Arms.** In the Alcazaba this area is named **Barrio Castrense,** or Military District, since it is, in essence, a small «city» within a city. This area has a trapezoid-shaped floor plan on which up to seventeen different residences were distributed, although all that remains today are the original buildings' foundations. Most of these dwellings had an upper floor, lavatory and even an inner court-yard. Especially outstanding is a residence of large di-mensions with an equally large number of rooms, that appears to have had a pool in its inner courtyard and even a hypocaust, probably used for heating the house. This would lead us to believe that it was the living-quarters for the Commander of the Guard. There were also storehouses, dormitory barracks for the junior sen-tries, a complete bath system and an Arab cistern (which is no longer preserved; the one that stands to-day was commissioned by the Catholic Monarchs).

The central axis of this small «city» is crossed by one main avenue, although the paths of other smaller streets are still visible. These ran in labyrinthian fashion from one residence to another, as was typical of Arab cities.

At the foot of the inner side of the great Broken To-wer (so-named for having been totally destroyed on se-veral occasions) and beneath the two massive blocks that protrude from the bulwark, there is a dungeon, or silo, depending on the purpose it was to serve, that opens up at subfloor level.

Besides the powerful eastern stretch of bulwark with

25

its three towers, the Military District is closed at its western end by two other fortified ramparts that converge at the **Torre de la Vela,** or Sentinel's Tower. At the northern section of the bulwark three small block towers rise just slightly above the parapet wall, and the far end leads to the spacious terrace of the Tower of Arms.

The southern wall, reconstructed several times, preserves just one small tower called the **Torre de la Sultana,** or Tower of the Sultana, at the foot of which stands a door that leads into the **Jardín de los Adarves** (or Garden of the Parapets). This garden dates from the 17th century when the moat to the south of the Al-

The Vermilion Towers.

cazaba was packed with earth up to the level of the parapet of the outer wall.

Continue on to the left, towards the west, cross through the **Torre de la Pólvora,** or Gunpowder Tower (notice the plaque that hangs on the outer façade bearing the testimonial verses of **Icaza**) to enter into the **Sentinel's Tower.**

The Tower has a cellar (probably used as a dungeon at one time) and four floors, each with a small central square hall contained within a narrow, square-shaped gallery. A rather steep, winding staircase leads up to the tower terrace where the impressive and uninterrupted panorama of the surrounding landscape spans before us: the «crest» of mountains that encircle the fertile Granada valley, dotted with quaint farming villages; the **Sierra Nevada Mountain** peaks, snow-covered in winter; the city of Granada and its different neighbourhoods —the **Albaicín, Sacromonte;** the **Cerro del Sol** (Hill of the Sun) with the **Silla del Moro** (Seat of the Moor) as its sentry; all this unfolds around us as though the Tower were an authentic diurnal planetarium, revolving on its own axis.

This Tower, with its hourly bell toll that used to mark the changes in irrigation in the Granada Valley until very recent times, was in essence the city's clock. For many centuries it was known as the **Tower of the Sun** since the equinox was visible on its main façade. Its majestic silhouette can still been seen from miles away, announcing the living presence of the city's symbol.

Returning to the first floor of the Sentinel's Tower, through the door and descending another two short flights of stairs, continue the tour of the Alcazaba at the Arab cistern located at the foot of the Tower. Then down another three steps and, to the left, through the remains of a gate belonging to the higher part of the enclosure. The gate preserves its magnificent brick vaulting and its marvellous outer stone façade and perfectly-proportioned horseshoe arch, considered to be the oldest piece in the whole of the Alhambra.

Down another steep hill, to the right under the external bulwark of the citadel wall, turn to the right again and continue as far as a cylindrical construction used for artillery to protect the «ram» of the Alhambra above the city of Granada. Here, behind a postern that is no longer preserved today, the sentries would begin their

The Gate of Arms.

patrol along the parapet wall that joined the **Alcazaba** with the **Vermilion Towers,** after making their rounds of what is known today as the **Cuesta de los Gómerez.**

Walking around practically the entire base of the **Sentinel's Tower,** both the magnitudes of its dimensions and its stateliness will be better appreciated. This route involves crossing what was probably a parapet walk protected by an exterior rampart highlighting the defensive character of the **Alcazaba**.

This leads into a small, elongated courtyard and on the left side stands a doorway to the **Caballerizas** or Stable Yards of the Alcazaba. This is a rectangular building with one central passage and alternating horse stalls with arched entrances on either side. Only the foundation base of the right nave remains since this part of the building was allowed to deteriorate on several occasions throughout its history. At the back of the Stable Yards rises the **Torre de los Hidalgos** (the Knight's Tower).

A small modern doorway opened in the rampart that used to close the **Stable Courtyard** to the north, and now leads to the outside of the Alhambra enclosure.

The **Tower of Arms** rises up from a steep roadway

Garden of the Parapets.

that descends to the left. The **Gate of Arms** was one of the four main entrances to the Alhambra. Its outer façade still preserves most of the magnificent tiles decorating the ashlars in the spandrel of its brick horseshoe arch. **Saint Peter's Woods** stretch before this Gate down to the banks of the **Darro River,** hiding what was once the medieval road from the city of Granada to the Alhambra.

The tracks for the characteristic portcullis, which would have been immediately lowered in a state of alert, can be seen at the jambs of the **Gate of Arms.**

Inside the gate, notice the typical Z-shaped passageway, the benches where the sentries used to sit and above all the alternating pattern of vaulting styles, again, characteristically painted red in imitation of exposed brick. The end of the Gate has a double, horseshoe-arched opening to either side: in medieval

times the right-hand opening led to the inside of the **Alcazaba.** A street, flanked on either side by ramparts, stemmed from the opening on the left which, after passing through a small square area with stone benches used by the knights for dismounting their horses, leads today's visitor to the inside of the Alhambra as it did the citizens of Granada during Arab times.

The **Round Tower** stands at the end of this street. From this point, visitors may appreciate the perfect protection and surveillance advantages offered by the superimposed stretches of bulwark. In the 1950's an excavation team uncovered the destroyed **Gate of the Flour Mill** which has been rebuilt under the small tower that served to protect it. The intervening spaces on either side of the horseshoe-arched Gate seem to represent an evocation suggestive of the two worlds sheltered by the Alhambra: the Christian, coarse and arrogant; and the Arab, sensitive and introvert.

The grand Palace Esplanade spans out on the other side of the Tower.

View of the Alcazaba Towers from the Square of the Arab Cisterns.

View of the Alhambra from the Albaicín quarter. ➤

The Comares Hall.

The Courtyard of the Myrtles.

THE PALACE ESPLANADE

To the north of the **Square of the Arab Cisterns,** between these and the main enclosure bulwark, a wide esplanade stretches out with the ruined remains of the original paving and foundation bases for several buildings.

The importance of this site has been proven through successive excavations. In medieval times this esplanade was a major junction of the Alhambra —the authentic communication centre between the different outbuildings— since the main avenues of the Alhambra converged, or rather stemmed, from this esplanade.

The citizens of Granada would come through the **Gate of Arms** to enter into the Alhambra, just like the present-day visitor. From here, a number of entrances were available. One being through a gate, now in ruins, that stood by the still existing drinking fountain, connected with the **Wine Gate** along a steep street. This street, formerly the route to the **Medina** (or city) of the Alhambra, is currently used as the main access for the tour through the **Nasrid Palaces.**

The Palace esplanade.

Alternatively, there was another gate next to this one, which formed a right angle with it and led to the other main avenue of the Alhambra known as the **Calle Real Baja** (or Lower Royal Avenue) that ran to the east.

Also on the esplanade rose the main façade of the **Arab Palace** protected by a now ruined counterwall.

Entrance to the Nasrid Palaces.

To the northeast, at the lowest part of the esplanade, stand the jambs which mark the position of a former gate which led to a **Surveillance Route.** From here sentries would patrol the entire Alhambra enclosure along the scarp of the citadel bulwark.

As would be expected of a public square, the espalanade still bears the remains of what were once small merchandise stalls embedded in the bulwark.

THE NASRID PALACES

As has been mentioned earlier, the ideal itinerary would start with the tour of the **Alcazaba** followed immediately afterwards by a visit to the **Palaces.** Nevertheless, should visitors care to make a special tour of the Palaces, access may be gained through the walkway that begins at the Wine Gate and runs down into the **Palace Esplanade.**

Of the seven Arab palaces identified as having once existed in the Alhambra, the buildings pertaining to only two, the **Comares** and the **Leones** Palaces, still stand intact. This excellent state of preservation is partially due to the fact that the Catholic Monarchs commissioned the two palaces for their private use, and joined them to form what has been called the **Old Royal Residence** standing opposite the **New Royal Residence,** or the **Charles V Palace.**

The Machuca Courtyard Gallery.

Between the **Esplanade** and the entrance to the **Comares Palace** lie two square-shaped courtyards that used to be considered outbuildings of the Palace, although it is more likely that they were used as the medieval court's administrative offices.

The first of these two courtyards (although only the remains are visible) contained an **oratory** and **minaret**, both duly facing **Mecca**, as well as a series of long alcove-like halls which overlooked the courtyard.

The northern wall of the second, called **Machuca's Courtyard**, still retains its magnificent nine-arched portico, and it seems likely that it originally stood facing a matching counterpart. This Courtyard is named after the celebrated architect-builder of the **Charles V Palace** who used it as his study.

The Mexuar.

A small look-out tower, with rich interior decoration, opens up out from the portico offering magnificent views of the surrounding landscape. In the middle of the courtyard lies a long pool, shaped in the likeness of the Roman **Water-Lily Ponds,** where two water-jets would fill the pool from either end.

Crossing through the remaining jambs of the gate at the southeast corner of the courtyard and up a short flight of stairs, lies the **Mexuar**. Here a fine façade gives way to the interiors of the building where the Council of Ministers to the Sultan, called the **Mexuar,** would congregate to discuss important affairs. This room has undergone a number of modifications, the most significant occurring in the 16th century when it was transformed into a chapel. This room must have originally been a square-shaped hall, where an illuminating lantern was hung from the centre of the area that surmounts the four columns that still stand in the centre. The present-day windows were installed to provide the chapel with light, as was the wooden balustrade that replaced the wall that once stood at the end of the room. Behind this dividing wall was a small courtyard that was a further addition to the chapel.

At the very back of the **Mexuar,** the wall closing a small oratory which overlooked the surrounding landscape was removed. Entrance to this oratory was originally from the **Machuca gallery.** It still preserves the characteristic **mihrab** facing the **Mecca,** although the floor was lowered considerably and the only reminder of the original can be seen in the small stone ledge found to the right of the string of open windows.

At the northeast corner of the **Mexuar** stands a small doorway crowned by a horseshoe arch leading into the **Cuarto Dorado** (or Gilded Room), that served as an important administrative office. The anteceding court-

Gilded Room gallery.

yard was used by the sultan to administer justice to his subjects. There were originally three windows that opened up to the outside that were replaced by the remaining central window, ornamented in a clearly **mudéjar** style. The coffered ceiling has been transformed accordingly, with Arab-style paintings interspersed with gold-painted emblems of the Catholic Monarchs, hence the name given to the room.

The portico with its three fine arches only partially retains the original lower decoration. Particularly outstanding are the central **Almohade** style capitals. Only the left-hand side of the outer courtyard still holds some pieces of its original smooth lime stucco.

The majestic outside façade of the **Comares Palace** rises up just opposite the **Gilded Room,** where the separation between administrative or governing duties and private family life is clearly distinguished. The building of the palace was decreed by **Muhammad V** in 1370 to celebrate the overthrow of the city of **Algeciras,** and, without a doubt, it constitutes one of the major Islamic architectural works.

Of the two doors, the one on the right led op to the sultan and his family's private apartments, and the door on the left was reserved for the sultan's official life, transforming into reality the symbolic inscription above the door: «My door is a parting of the ways».

The sultan would receive his subjects before the outer façade. From his slightly elevated position as he stood on the three steps, he would appear framed by the splendour of the façade crowned by beautiful wooden eaves (a masterpiece of Islamic art). The multi-coloured decoration (a common motif in Nasrid art) that once imbued the façade and deepened in hue as it rose upwards, acquired symbolic dimensions.

As a reminder of the distance to be kept between outsiders and the sultan's private affairs, it is a left-handed door which connects the Palace to the **Patio de los Arrayanes** (or Courtyard of the Myrtles) up through a Z-shaped passageway. This passageway was closed by two doors that opened in different directions to further protect the privacy of the sultan's apartments as well as to prevent escape should any intruder find his way in.

Down one of the side corridors of the Courtyard of

South gallery in the Courtyard of the Myrtles.

the Myrtles (receiving its name from its two luxuriant beds of myrtles) head towards the portico located on the left. From the threshold of the doorway, the central axis of the Courtyard and the high façade at the opposing end dominate the view. Behind the visitor, lies the entrance to the Palace's main halls.

First is the **Hall of the Barca**, meaning, «**baraka**» or blessing in Arabic, intercepted at either end by arches that frame two dormitory alcoves. A small horseshoe-arched doorway in the alcove on the left leads to a lavatory that dates from the 14th century. In the alcove to the right a doorway was opened to connect the Christian servants' quarters with the **Royal Residence**. The beautiful wood ceiling crowning the hall is a reconstructed version of the original which was partially destroyed when a fire broke out in the late 19th century.

Further on, at the next threshold before entering the adjoining **Sala del Trono** (Hall of the Throne), are two short, narrow passageways. The one on the left leads to the Palace tower stairway (where winter quarters are located); the one to the right leads to a small **oratory** whose **mihrab** was perforated during Christian times.

The **Hall of the Throne,** also known as the **Comares Hall** or **the Ambassador's Hall,** is the Palace's main room and the largest in the Alhambra. It takes up the whole of the inside area of the great 45 m tower, that protrudes out from the bulwark wall and can be seen from miles around. The bulwark walls have been hollowed out around the Hall, forming nine small alcoves that look out onto open country. These are arranged in opposing pairs excepting the one aligned with the doorway. The central alcoves were reserved for the sultan and their decoration is quite exceptional and unique.

Without doubt the most remarkable feature of the Hall is its impressive ceiling timbering, originally very vividly coloured, and made up of an intricate webbing of minute geometrical pieces, cleverly achieving a three dimensional depth by overlapping planes. Besides being a decorative architectural element, it also represents an entire Arab treatise on eschatology. The ceiling symbolically represents the Seven Heavens of Islam that ascend and revolve around an eighth firmament —the Islamic god's dwelling place— represented in the ceiling by a small central honey-combed cupola that appears to legitimize and protect the sultan's throne.

All of the paraments in the room display rich gypsum plaster decorations, which were once brightly coloured and some of their elements painted in the finest detail and delicacy worthy of a miniaturist, with intricate and magnificently splendid designs sheathing the tiled socles —one of the most outstanding rooms in the Alhambra.

Of the Hall's original flooring, only a small square section remains in the centre of the room to which several pieces were later added. The balcony at the first alcove to the right, at the very entrance to the room, was converted into a doorway. Thus the other buildings built on to the Arab Palace by the Catholic Monarchs for their own **Royal Residence,** became connected. The two extremely diverse **Comares** and **Leones** Palaces were literally made into one.

The four ground-floor summer residences with their characteristic horseshoe arches are located on either side of the **Courtyard of the Myrtles.** The beautiful gypsum plaster decorations stand out against the relatively monotonous side wall. Next to these impressive arches are other smaller ones that gave access to the four corresponding **algorfas** or winter chambers located on the upper floor. The only exceptions being the doorway at the central portion of the west gallery, which was a service door, and the doorway found immediately next to the north portico, which leads to the **Palace baths.** The **algorfas** of the four upper residences open up into the courtyard by means of several double-arched windows with mullion and lattice wood coverings.

A large, mirror-like pool (34.70 m by 7.15 m) fills the centre of the courtyard, fulfilling an aesthetic function since it not only breaks the horizontal line of the courtyard but also adds greater depth and erectness, especially noticeable from either of the short sides of the courtyard.

At the south end of the Courtyard, behind the portico, a door leads into another hall resembling the Hall of the Barca, although somewhat smaller. This hall, today leading to the **Crypt** of the **Charles V Palace,** was named the **Hall of the Aleyas** since it bore decorative inscriptions from the Koran that were later transferred elsewhere. During the building of the Crypt the whole southern wall, which closed off the **Comares Palace,** was demolished.

Over the portico there is a another hall that opens out onto the courtyard with seven windows, the central one having a double arch and mullion. All of the windows bear beautiful lattice woodwork coverings. The top floor of the building is crowned by an open gallery that also overlooks the courtyard. A square linteled opening stands in the middle of the six arches which frame the gallery.

The **Catholic Monarchs** connected the **Comares Palace** to the **Palace of the Lions** cutting through the dividing wall behind the small doorway that had served as access to the upper southeast residence. The Monarchs made a further entrance to the Palace of the Lions through one of the southernmost ground floor residences.

Comares Palace
façade.

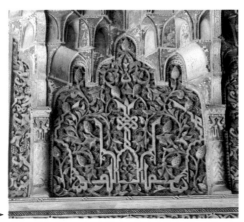

Courtyard of the
Myrtles and Comares
Tower.

➜

THE PALACE OF THE LIONS

Palace of the Lions.

The **Palace of the Lions** was built during the reign of **Muhammad V** (1354-59 and 1362-91), at the culmination of the Nasrid sultanate. The whole of the Palace forms a single, independent unit within the palatial core of the Alhambra. While its present-day entrance was remodelled by the Christians, the original ones were lo-

cated both in the **Sala de los Mocárabes** (Hall of the **mocárabes** —honey-comb relief or multifaceted diadems—) and in the **Sala de los Reyes** (the Hall of Kings). The first of these two halls had a doorway through to the **Lower Royal Avenue,** and the **Hall of Kings** led to the **Partal Gardens** through a beautiful building with a magnificent cupola known by the misleading name of **La Rauda** (or Arab cemetery).

The Palace ground floor includes all that was considered essential in a traditional Hispano-Arab residence: separate summer and winter quarters with multifunctional alcoves encircling a central open courtyard. Nevertheless, a transept courtyard was adopted for this Palace (a style used elsewhere, both in **Al-Andalus** and in the **East**) and was considered to be the Palace's most outstanding feature, since it achieved the greatest perfection in concept, development and proportions.

The Palace holds a vestibular hall —the Hall of the **Mocárabes**—, two independent residences (the Hall of the **Abencerrajes,** or Arab Courtiers, and the Hall of the Two Sisters), both double-storey constructions, and a hall for meetings or social gatherings (**Sala de los Re-**

The Hall of Two Sisters.

yes, or Hall of Kings), clearly reflecting the hierarchical nature of the Arab court. All these halls lead off from the Courtyard, in the centre of which stands the **Fountain of the Lions.** The **Patio de Lindaraja** (or Courtyard of the Scenic Lookout), which now occupies the original lower garden, caused the garden's complete defacement and even the disappearance of the Palace bath.

The appearance that the **Courtyard of the Lions** offers today is very different from former days. The four, earth-filled flower beds marked out by the arms of the transept configuration were at a lower level with respect to the narrow walkways and galleries, thus emphasising the depth and erectness of the Courtyard with its symmetrical lines converging at the fountain.

The **fountain,** symbol of the Palace, was probably a creation based on one of the Biblical narrations about the **Bronze Sea** or the **Temple of Jerusalem,** substituting the twelve bulls for twelve lions. The ingenious water supply system allowed the fountain to maintain a constant water level that was beautifully explained

The Hall of Kings.

and praised by the suggestive metaphors sculpted on the outer ridge of the fountain's basin. These metaphors, in twelve verses, were the work of the **Visir** (one of the Mexuar counsellors) and the poet **Ibn Zamrak.**

As its name indicates, the **Hall of the Mocárabes,** the first room encountered upon entering the Palace, used to boast a vault decorated with **mocárabes,** or multifaceted diadems. The explosion of a nearby powderkeg in 1590 caused extensive damage to this fragile vault which was later replaced in the 17th century by the present-day one.

The **mocárabe** vaults in the **Hall of the Arab Courtiers** to the southern end, and in the **Hall of the Two Sisters** to the northern end, are masterpieces of Islamic art. Based on the **Pythagoras Theorem,** a central star spreads geometrically over a three-dimensional plane complemented by a rich and vari-coloured finish. The sunlight throughout the day further enhances its range of hues with play of light and shadows accentuated by its three-dimensional relief.

The Hall of Two Sisters. →

The Halls of both the **Arab Courtiers** and the **Two Sisters** are on a slightly higher plane than the Courtyard, emphasising their function as independent residences. Just inside the entrances to both halls, there are two narrow passageways that lead to a lavatory on one side and to the upper floor stairway on the other. The most remarkable of the large number of upper-floor rooms were those that looked out onto the Courtyard through three beautiful frontal arches. The **Hall of the Arab Courtiers** has no opening to the outside other than the main entrance and the windows surrounding the cupola. Two central areas converging at a twelve-sided marble fountain in the middle of the room open up into two side alcoves surmounted by a double arch. The socles skirting the Hall are covered with Sevillian ceramic tiles dating from the 16th century.

The two alcoves on either side of the **Hall of the Two Sisters** originally had windows opening to the outside, although the left alcove window was later converted into a door. This Hall opened into another, called the **Sala de los Ajimeces** (or Hall of the Double Arch Column Windows) which extends further into the **Mirador de Lindaraja** (the Scenic Lookout Tower) that juts out over the Palace's lower garden. As is obvious from its name, this Tower used to look out over the surrounding landscape. It has the most refined decorations in the Palace, particularly noteworthy are the tiny intrados ceramic tiles covering the socles, the gypsum plaster that frames the windows and coloured glass ceiling.

The **Hall of Kings** was the Palace's main room, clearly intended for court events and entertainment purposes. Three alcoves open up along the wall facing the Courtyard, each surmounted by vaults covered with miniaturist-style representations painted on leather. The theme of the paintings over the left alcove tells of the fight between a Christian and Arab knight for the hand of a maiden, and how, following successive competitions, the Arab knight gains his victory. The painting above the central alcove tells of a meeting of important authorities.

The square-shaped building known as **La Rauda** (or Arab Cemetery), was probably part of a former palace. On each side there is a horseshoe arch and an upper block of windows, covered by an inner ovolo cupola over squinches, again painted in imitation of traditional exposed red brick. This fine building must have served as a majestic exit to the **Partal Gardens,** for the private use of the sultan and his guests.

THE PARTAL GARDENS

From the **Rauda,** enter the terraced **Partal Gardens** that appear to have covered the numerous archeological remains, fountains, pools, narrow walkways and walls that have been uncovered since the beginning of this century. The Gardens descend in terraces, leading to an open square. This is a central starting point for tours of the **Comares Palace Baths**, the **Palace of the Partal**, the **Puerta del Arrabal** (or Gate to the Outside) and the **Generalife**.

At the highest part of the Gardens is a rest area where guide books or souvenirs are on sale. From here the tour may be continued, either towards the ruins of the **Palace of Yusuf III** or towards the **Royal Avenue** and the general exit from the Alhambra enclosure.

The Partal Gardens.

LINDARAJA AND THE COMARES BATH

From the esplanade at the lowest part of the **Partal Gardens** there is a short pergola leading down to the inside of the **Lindaraja Courtyard.** This is the Christian building of the lower garden belonging to the **Palace of the Lions** whose look-out tower, which has given this whole section its name, majestically presides over the courtyard.

The modification by the Christians meant closing off the Courtyard that originally looked out on to the surrounding landscape, as though it were a cloister. The Courtyard is now surrounded by galleries on the lower

The Lindaraja Courtyard.

floor while the upper floor has living quarters. Most of the columns, bases and capitals found in the lower gallery have been transferred from other parts of the Alhambra.

A Baroque fountain made from Elvira Sierra stone stands in the centre of the Courtyard and is crowned by the original ovolo fountain from the Arab garden, bearing a beautiful poetic inscription around the fountain rim.

At the back of the Courtyard, through an arbour open in the wall that once closed the garden, stands the **Patio de la Reja** (The Iron Gate Courtyard), thus named because of the beautiful wrought iron work that closes the upper rooms of the **Comares Bath** where the royal crockery was stored after the Conquest. This Courtyard looks out onto the landscape from its northern side where there is a two-tiered gallery bridge built by the

Hall of Repose in the Comares Palace Bath.

Christians to join the **Comares Hall** directly to the Emperor's rooms. The Courtyard's location and its open corridors make it an ideal resting place while contemplating the scenic panorama. The galleries are supported by columns and capitals taken from other parts, and some are authentic masterpieces. Off the upper gallery an antechamber leads to the Emperor's study, a somewhat larger room with a beautiful ceiling and stone chimney piece.

In the antechamber, above the door adjacent to the study, a marble plaque reminds visitors that these are the rooms used by the celebrated author of **The Tales of the Alhambra, Washington Irving.** These rooms house both furniture and ornamental objects from different periods. The chimney piece and the richly decorated ceilings are among the most prized pieces, and especially outstanding is the ceiling of the **Sala de las Frutas** (Hall of the Fruits).

There is access from the study antechamber to an open gallery that connects this section of the building

Clerestory windows in the Comares Palace Bath.

with the upper floor of a tower called the **Peinador de la Reina** (or the Queen's Dressing Room). In the 16th century, the upper floor of this tower or Arab kiosk was converted into a delightful lookout tower. The interior decoration, mostly frescos dating from the 16th century, contrast beautifully with the Nasrid decoration dating from the 14th century_of the lower floor, in a strange symbosis of a decorative zenith of two radically different worlds.

Returning to the **Patio de la Reja,** a spacious area originally led to a water mains supply behind which is visible the impressive vaulted cellar of the **Comares Palace,** traditionally given the name of the **Sala de la Ninfas** (or Hall of the Nymphs), where the sultan's treasure chamber was supposedly located.

Today visitors enter the **Comares Bath** from this point, since the original entrance at the **Courtyard of the Myrtles** has undergone numerous modifications.

The **Sala de las Camas** (or Hall of Repose) lies at the end of a zig-zag passageway containing a bench covered in ceramic tiling dating from the 16th century. Despite the modifications in the interior decoration, whimsically repainted during the reign of Elizabeth II, the hall still preserves the magic of its purpose, a place of repose and corporal attentions before the bath. The room was lit by a hanging lantern, and the rooms immediately above were reserved for the bath servants. Since the bath belonged to the Palace, these servants enjoyed a high social status. The door opposite the entrance leads to the bath lavatory. On the same wall, another door leads to a staircase giving direct access to the **Courtyard of the Myrtles,** and a fourth door leads to the bath's steam chambers.

Star-shaped skylights in Comares Palace Bath.

Comares Bath steam room. →

These chambers are surmounted by vaults with perforated glazed vents, serving as skylights that the servants would open or close to regulate the steam in the halls. Underneath the marble flooring and on the inside

53

of the walls, conduits of varing diameters heated the halls by means of the hot steam and air produced by the water furnaces, from which the water filled the bath basins at will through double spouts for hot and cold water respectively.

The largest hall in this bath, with a twin triple-arched arcade, was the warmest and where some type of thick foot covering was necessary so as to avoid burning one's feet. To one end another hall opens with two large bath basins standing opposite the entrance made in Christian times to give direct access to the **Calderas** (or Boiler Room). The 16th century modernisations are noticeable in the ceramic socles and the cellar entrance door to the **Hall of the Two Sisters,** whose central vault produces echoes that gave rise to its name: the **Sala de los Secretos** (or Hall of Secrets).

Leaving behind the **Lindaraja Courtyard,** head once again towards the **Partal Gardens.**

Detailed feature of column in the Hall of Repose.

THE PALACE OF THE PARTAL

The lowest terrace of the **Partal Gardens** holds a large pool presided over by the grand five-arched portico of an important palace. The attribution of the construction of this Palace to **Muhammad II** is based on the remains that have been preserved, and on its decoration —making it the oldest palace of the palatine area of the **Alhambra.**

The Partal Palace.

This Palace has several differentiating characteristics. The portico opens onto a garden, with no side nave extension or front gallery, typical features of this type of building. It is unlikely that a courtyard ever existed. However, intringuing little houses seem to be attached to the western wing that preserve their interior tempera paintwork. To the east side there is an isolated oratory slightly raised above the palace which, even if only the decoration, was supposedly commissioned by **Yusuf I.**

The **Torre de las Damas** (or Tower of the Ladies-in-Waiting) protrudes from behind the portico gallery over the **Darro River** basin, central point of the palace. Its chamber is a magnificent lookout that contains the oldest decorative remains of the **Alhambra.**

Slightly higher up and to one side of the portico rises

a beautiful building that bas been called **«the observatory»** as well as a «dovecote».

Two large lions sit at the far end of the large pool which originally belonged to the 16th-century **Hospital del Maristán** (the Maristan Hospital), once located in the **Albaicín** but now demolished.

It seems unlikely that the ruined remains of the buildings opposite the palatine residence, rising in terraces within the **Partal Gardens** ever formed part of the Palace grounds. A residence facing and resembling the portico, however, may have existed. It is also possible that in the periods following the Palace's construction its original lay-out was reformed, leaving the portico untouched and integrating it into an open garden as it is seen today.

The lower part of the **Partal Gardens** rises in layers,

The Partal Gardens.   *The Rauda Gate.*

built in modern-times to camouflage the ruined remains of medieval constructions which, in turn, contributed to the unique nature and organisation of the Gardens, further enchanced by the beauty of its location.

To either continue the route or leave the grounds, visitors should walk up to the highest terrace of the **Gardens.** The route which follows the double staircase opposite the portico and behind the statues of the lions is particularly enchanting for its scenery and contrasts. It crosses the remains of a small pavillion surrounded by two right-angle pools followed by a courtyard with a central pool.

To the eastern end of the lower terrace stems a street leading towards the **Torre de los Picos** (or Tower of the Spurred Merlons). At the foot of the tower stands the so-called **Puerta del Arrabal** (or Gate to the Outside), one of the four entrances to the **Alhambra.** An extensive stable yard stretches out, connected to the **Gate of Iron** that led to the medieval entrance to the **Generalife.**

REST AREA

The magnificent views and refreshing shade offered by the highest terrace of the **Partal Gardens** make this an ideal spot for a rest before resuming the visit. Bench seating and refreshments are available, and guide books, souvenirs, slides and films are on sale at the stand.

The exit from the Alhambra grounds goes from the rest area, down an avenue that passes by the Royal

Rest area in the Generalife.

Rest area in the Partal Gardens.

Cemetery or the **Rauda** and to the left towards the **Royal Avenue,** bordering the east and south façade of the Charles V Palace.

The visit, however, may be continued from the opposite end of the rest area.

PALACE OF YUSUF III

Through a courtyard flanked on one side by the ruined remains of what were once residences, and with a small central pool, the route enters a lengthy garden surrounding a long narrow pool, forming the central point of the Palace of Yusuf III.

The Palace was traditionally known by the names of **Palace of Mondéjar** or **Palace of Tendilla.** These names originate from the time when the Catholic Monarchs ceded the palatial building to its first occupant, Mondéjar, and it was successively used as the residence for the **alcaides** (or mayors) of the Alhambra, until Phillip V stripped them of this right and ordered the premises to be vacated in 1718. In retaliation the Palace's former occupants ordered its demolition, selling anything and everything they could columns, doors...

The Palace was built by **Yusuf III** (1408-1417) when the most important palaces already built in the Alhambra were at the height of their splendour. The influence in lay-out and design is apparent since the ground plan, although smaller in scale, greatly resembles that of the **Courtyard of the Myrtles.**

The location of the Palace is admirable, at the highest

Tour of the Towers.

Outside view of Towers and parapet.

part of the **Partal Gardens.** The centre tower, of which only several low walls remain, must have reached far above the palace gardens and other buildings, combining excellent views of the surrounding panorama while at the same time serving as an exceptional lookout tower for defence purposes.

Close to the large rectangular courtyard and its central pool (6 m wide by at least 27 m long), lie the barely visible remains of several other apartments located to the north, around the tower. A continuous gallery, with a portico fringed with a series of arches, similar to the other courtyards found in the Alhambra, probably ran around the inside of the apartments.

At a slightly lower level on either side of the palace grounds other ruins have been found of buildings that probably belonged to the Palace. At the extreme southeast stood the Palace bath and adjoining rooms, repeating the familiar characteristic pattern of this type of building: hypocaust, basins and several water channels are still easily recognisable.

The remains of further palace apartments are still in evidence to the north of the **Bath,** surrounding an almost square courtyard which might well have been one of the entrances. This conjecture is based on the discovery of the remains of a wide doorway in front of which cobbled paths, marking several streets connecting to other parts of the Alhambra, were unearthed.

Stripped of its rich decorative elements little was left to attract passers-by which explains why the grounds were abandoned to the mercy of the weather, half-buried under their own ruins. Today they have become mere archeological witnesses to the **Alhambra's** past.

THE TOWERS

From the ruined remains of the **Palace of Yusuf III** several landscaped gardens stretch out to the east, from where the visit of the **Alhambra** may be continued.

These gardens overlook the whole of the inner side of the Alhambra enclosure bulwark, which in turn, stands above the patrol route running along the scarp, also known as the **Foso** (or moat) since it could be used as such. Towers stand at irregular intervals along another sentinal route, named the **Adarve** (or parapet walk) which runs along the bulwark wall. These towers served not only as watch towers, but also as residences for important personalities, most probably related in some way or another to the sentries.

Tour of the Towers.

The first of these towers is called the **Torre de los Picos** (Tower of the Spurred Merlons), so named for the shape of the battlements projecting from the upper part of the tower's corners, which remain as evidence of the reforms the tower underwent during the Christian period. Several decorative items are still visible inside the tower, particularly noteworthy are a number of beautiful paintings that decorate the vault surmounting the tower's main room. This tower presided over one of the four entrances to the **Alhambra** —the **Gate to the Outside** which is found at the foot of the Tower.

The next tower, although of lesser proportions, is known by the name of **Candil** or **del Cadí** (the Oil-Lamp Tower), and in olden days was also referred to as the «fox pass». This also served as a watch tower, since

Tower of the Princesses.

it sits just on the border of the medieval entrance to the **Generalife** grounds.

This entrance resembles a corridor winding through the gardens until it reaches the plateau on the neighbouring hill where the majestic white buildings of the garden palace stand.

A garden can still be discerned towards the right, inside the Alhambra. This once belonged to a former Arab Palace which was transformed into a **Franciscan Convent.** Today the buildings visible at the highest point of the hill house the **St. Francis Parador Hotel.** A protruding block still remains which was formerly part of the Palace's lookout tower, converted into a chapel following the Christian Conquest. It was on this site that the remains of the Catholic Monarchs were buried until work on the **Royal Chapel,** where they are buried today, was finalised.

The next tower along the bulwark wall is **la Cautiva** (Tower of the Captive Lady), considered a tower-palace due to its delicate decorations and the lay-out of the rooms' inside. Crossing over a wide bridge that spans the scarp of the sentry patrol route, a Z-shaped passageway leads into a small courtyard, surrounded by beautifully decorated hall-like galleries that open to upper floors with small, but graciously proportioned, windows that provided the courtyard with light.

Besides the rich gypsum plaster friezes, particularly outstanding are the ceramic tile socles next to the windows and covering the main hall, crowned by an inscription in blue on white background.

The **Torre de las Infantas** (or Tower of the Princesses) is situated at a slightly higher area and is of larger proportions. Its basic lay-out scheme is almost a duplicate of the previous tower-palace, although it was built later. Entrance to the tower is made through a Z-shaped passageway surmounted by a magnificent, painted imitation of an exposed red-brick vault. The tower courtyard, with a smal fountain in the centre, was originally covered by a **mocárabe** vault that has since been destroyed and replaced by the present-day ceiling timbering. Three side alcoves open up onto the courtyard, the central one being the most outstanding, with the typical recesses at each entrance. A number of alcoves on the upper floor look out onto the courtyard through large double-arched windows with mullion.

The stretch of bulwark that joined this Tower to the

Torre del Agua (or Water Tower) guarded the **Acequia Real** (or the Royal Irrigation Channels) entrance to the **Alhambra.** A massive doorway was recently built permitting access to and from the Alhambra from the Generalife over the modern **Puente Nuevo** (or New Bridge).

The Acequia Courtyard of the Generalife. ➤

The Partal Oratory.

THE GENERALIFE

The **Generalife** was probably the most outstanding estate to stretch along the area surrounding the Alhambra, proof of which is found in the superb palace decorations.

The Generalife was conceived as a leisure estate, with an area of palatine character and stretches of land intended for grazing and farming (at least four vegetable and fruit gardens have been identified). From present knowledge, it can be assumed that there was a section of fruit tree orchards, arable gardens for growing pod and leafy vegetables, cereales, etc., and pastures for both farm animals and for the horses bred at the sultan's stable.

Of the four vegetable and fruit gardens that have

The Generalife Gardens.

been identified, at least one is still farmed. The name of the original four are **Colorada** (or the Coloured Garden), the **Grande** (or Great Garden), the **Fuentepeña** and the **Mercería** (or the Haberdasher's Garden). Even though these name were assigned to the gardens during the Christian period, for the most part they probably refer to their medieval counterparts. These gardens spread out in terraces below the palace that majestically presided over the surrounding area. The lookout tower in (wer in) the **Courtyard of the Acequia** is by far the most splendid component. The gardens extended as far as the **Cuesta de los Chinos,** that formed a valley bed between the gardens and the foothills of the **Alhambra,** all of which were enclosed by retaining and separating

walls, some of which can still be distinguished today.

The Generalife.

The notion of nature, either as part of the landscape or as part of the gardens, surpasses and overshadows any other impression the **Generalife** can evoke. The elimination or conversion of buildings effected on the estate contribute greatly to this impression. These changes were made for two reasons: firstly owing to the radically different Muslim and Christian living and leisure styles, and secondly, to the long and continued use of the estate as a private property until 1921.

In medieval times, the **Generalife** had at least two outer entrances. One led to the **Alhambra** citadel through the **Gate of Iron** along the **Cuesta de los Chinos,** at the foot of the **Tower of the Spurred Merlons.** This access route, preserved to this day in its original state, rose towards the Palace by way of a small street intersecting the gardens and protected by walls, leading into the same courtyard from which the tour of the Palace begins today.

The other outer entrance to the **Generalife** was located at what is known today as the **Mimbre** (or Osier Bed), next to the **Fuentepeña** parking area. This entrance has undergone numerous transformations, the most important being the creation of a wide **Paseo de Cipreses** (or Cypress Walk), reformed in 1862 for Elizabeth II's visit.

Access to the **Generalife** can also be found today at the recently-constructed **New Bridge** that connects the eastern end of the walled **Alhambra** enclosure to the **Cypress Walk.**

The spacious area that serves as a walkway to the Palace entrance (a former part of the estate's gardens in medieval times) was radically altered during this century by the creation of several pleasantly appointed gardens, as well as an open-air theatre. It in this incomparable setting that the **International Festival of Music and Dance** is held annually.

The entrance to the **Generalife Palace** is through a courtyard called the **Descabalgamiento** (or the Courtyard for Dismounting) as there are several benches that

Aerial view of the Generalife.

were used for dismounting a horse after entering the Palace doors. This courtyard has two side naves that were probably used by the stable hands. In the middle, a door opens to reveal the sentry guards' benches. Above the door there is a windowed chamber, probably intented for surveillence and protection of the entrance.

A second courtyard serves as a link between the different levels of the entrance. The courtyard is flanked on either side by arched galleries and has a small fountain in its centre. The main entrance to the Palace, with a beautiful marble and ceramic façade presides over the whole courtyard.

Through a small Z-shaped passageway lined with benches for the sentries, rises a steep, narrow staircase that leads up to the heart of the Palace, namely

the **Acequia Courtyard.** This long, rectangular area is crossed in the centre by the water channels from the **Royal Acequia,** converting it into a transept-shaped courtyard. In 1959, remains were found of a small, central square and the original garden, that was divided into four octagonal flower beds surrounded by slightly raised pathways.

The Generalife Gardens.

Twelve conduits have been preserved in the **Royal Acequia** channel walls, seven of which still retain their original Arab piping for irrigation. The whole system was modernised in the 19th century and the crossed fountain jets that have made the garden so popular were installed.

Originally the **Acequia Courtyard** did not overlook the landscape. In Christian times, a long, narrow corridor was opened allowing for some beautiful views of

Entrance to the Generalife Palace.

the scenic panorama. In the intrados of the arches tha connect the corridor with the courtyard, a painting o the Catholic Monarchs' coat of arms still hangs, bear ing its yoke and arrows, and the motto of the tw Spanish rulers indicating the equal division of authorit among the two («Tanto monta...»).

The only original opening of the courtyard to the out side is the small lookout tower located at the centra point of the enclosure, that still preserves the embra sure of the lower level windows. This typical feature o Islamic architecture allowed the Muslims to view the landscape from a sitting position.

On the other longer side of the Palace stand two ad jacent residences, both with lower hall and upper floor They resemble those found in the **Courtyard of the Myrtles** although smaller in size.

At the back of the courtyard is the **Sala Regia** (or Royal Hall) presided over by a wide, five-arched portico with a wider central arch, characteristic of Nasrid architecture. Both apartments, joined by a triple arch supported by slender columnettes and **mocárabe** capitals, have beautiful gypsum plasterwork and ceiling timbering, particularly in the gallery.

At the beginning of the 14th century, the lookout tower that projects over the **Darro River** bed was added, offering magnificent views of the city of Granada, the **Albaicín** and **Sacromonte**.

The building once had an upper floor built on by the **Catholic Monarchs** which was later engulfed by a wide open gallery that disfigured the whole of the building.

Successive adaptations have extensively altered the front façade of the Courtyard. It probably once had a central arch surmounted by a balcony overhanging the Courtyard, but this too has been modified.

From the **Royal Hall,** through a door and staircase opened to one side during Christian times, access is gained to the Palace's other buildings; from here onwards all the structures have been greatly modified.

The Courtyard of the Sultana's Cypress.

The adjoining **Patio del Ciprés de la Sultana** (or Courtyard of the Sultana's Cypress), setting for many mythic legends of romance, departs radically from the Muslim character.

A Baroque fountain surrounded by a U-shaped pool crossed with fountain water jets is found in the centre of the courtyard that then opens up into a two-tiered arbour-type gallery, built between 1584 y 1586.

At the other end, through the so-called **Puerta de los Leones** (Gate of the Lions) and up a steep staircase, access is made to the Palace's **Jardines Altos** (or High Gardens), also modified to better accommodate Western tastes.

Bordering the upper part of the wall surrounding the **Courtyard of the Sultana's Cypress,** lies the foot of the **Cascade Stairway,** last Arab vestige of the **Generalife.** Here the present-day visitor, just as the sultan did, walks up three flights of stairs under the natural vault formed by the foliage of bay leaves. The murmur of the cool water from the **Royal Acequia** that runs down the channels on either side of the stairway, creates a relaxed, peaceful atmosphere.

The stairway leads to the highest part of the Generalife, where a romantic lookout balcony was built in the 19th century; some of the best views are to be afforded from this point.

Under a pergola descends a modern staircase to the lower gardens. At these gardens there is a lookout over the **Acequia Courtyard,** also with magnificent views.

The **Puerta de la Mercería** (Haberdashery Gate) or **Puerta de los Carneros** (Gate of the Rams) stands at the end of this garden, and leads to the beginning of the **Paseo de las Adelfas** (the Oleander Walk). A rest area with beautiful views of the **Alhambra** is found at a small square behind. Before it lie the ruined remains of the **Casa de los Amigos** (The Friends' House) on a lower plane, one of the destroyed Palace buildings.

The **Oleander Walk,** so-named for the beautiful foliage of this plant which shades the walkway, is the final stage on the route of the Generalife tour. At the end it merges into the **Cypress Walk,** walkway which leads down to the **Fuentepeña** area.

THE CHRISTIAN ALHAMBRA

THE CHARLES V PALACE

The **Catholic Monarchs,** having received the Alhambra intact, with no battle scars or blemishes, bequeathed the grounds to their successors with only the modifications that were absolutely necessary to accommodate its Christian occupants. They had incorporated new features to the already exisiting Arab ones, without obliterating them, merely to mark the change in ownership.

Main façade of the Palace.

It was this modified version of the Alhambra that awaited **Charles I of Spain** (or **Charles V of Germany**). During his visit to the Alhambra in 1526, however, the King found it insufficient for his court. He was accompanied on this visit by his wife, Princess Isabel of Portugal, who was obliged to take up residence at the **St. Jerome Monastery.** Charles V intended to convert Granada into a residence fitting not for a king, but for an emperor, and it was therefore necessary to build an area, with new apartments and facilities, appropriate for the Renaissance court.

The Emperor did not destroy the great medieval buildings; only one hall of the **Comares Palace,** one similar to the **Hall of the Boat,** was affected. He estab-

75

lished the new Palace over an area that had been inhabited by the poorer Christians; an area that had only been used after the Christian Conquest. In reality he had wanted the new building and all its courtyards and façades to serve as a noble portico to the **Nasrid Palaces.** With this new construction he endowed Granada with its first royal palace for Christian monarchs.

The project, which was never completed or attained its aspirations, was commended to the painter, sculptor and architect, **Pedro Machuca.** He had studied in Italy under Michaelangelo and was thus well acquainted with the Renaissance tendencies of which he proved to be a pioneer in Spain. He began building in 1527, financed by the taxes imposed upon the Arab converts to Christianity.

Inner courtyard of the Charles V Palace.

The ground floor of the Palace attracts the visitor's attention since square rooms of varying dimensions

Southern façade of the Palace.

were distributed around the inner circular façade in such a manner that they still formed a square on the outside.

The Chapel, with an octagonal ground plan, breaks up this circle-square duality at the northeast corner. Examples similar to Machuca's idea had been seen before both in Spain and throughout Europe, particularly in Italy. A symbolic interpretation has been attributed to this geometrical configuration, namely the victory of Christian Europe over Islamic Europe, with subtle nuances hinting at Imperial unity and tradition.

Since the **Charles V Palace** is embedded in the **Comares Palace,** two of its four façades are more exquisitely decorated than the others. These are the southern and western façades, the latter being the Palace's main wall, both of which are arranged identically. The marmoreal doorways, standing rather like triumphal arches, are the main differentiating feature.

The main façade of the Palace is divided into two parts: firstly by a cornice that accentuates the width, further enhanced by the bench that runs along the entire lower part of the façade in plinth-like fashion, and secondly by the Corinthian cornice that garnishes the upper section. The pilasters, aligned directly one above the other in either section, afford a sensation of greater height, and frame the open rectangular spans topped by their rounded moulding.

The bevelled ashlars covering the whole of the outer façade are particularly remarkable. Several large bronze rings held by either bronze lion or eagle heads are encrusted in the pilaster ashlars.

The Courtyard of the Lions.

→

The decorative patterns on the upper section alternate in the emblems covering plinths resting on pilasters and in the edging on the shouldered arches of the balconies which form pediments. The Manneristic garlands strung across the window recesses further accentuate the horizontal plane of the façade. Another feature of Mannerism can be seen in the round moulding framing the pediments.

The southern double-doorway is framed by two pairs of columns standing on a frieze-ornamented base and pedestal. The large door is flanked by Ionic pilasters and crowned by a triangular pediment over which recline statuettes representing Victory. The above-mentioned pairs of columns are also Ionic in style. The frieze on the base and pedestal represent ancient and contemporary weapons; the base and pedestal continue along both sides of the façade to support two stone lions. The two upper pairs of Corinthian columns stand on a base and pedestal decorated with a mythological frieze which partially extends across the inner part of the doorway to decorate the support for the central arched structure.

The main doorway on the western façade is composed of an upper and lower section, as is the whole Palace. Here the pairs of half-columns accentuate the building's vertical plane. The lower semicolumns stand on a frieze-ornamented base and pedestal, forming symmetrical pairs. Worthy of special mention are those friezes depicting disarmament which equate the Palace to an **Ara Pacis.** A large central door and two smaller side doors are found in this section. The upper semicolumns stand on a base and pedestal which replace the sculptural ornamentation for symbols and cupids.

This doorway is the present-day entrance to the Palace's inner courtyard. A Z-shaped passageway, one of the three in the Palace, bearing Manneristic motifs, leads directly up to the courtyard.

The circular inner courtyard is surrounded by a two-tiered gallery. The lower gallery is surmounted by an undecorated annular, or ring-shaped, stone vault which was probably to have been painted with frescos. The 32 pilasters (with arches, doorways and niches opening between them) support the vaulting and stand in direct alignment with Tuscan-style Doric columns made of gravel granite. This is the courtyard's only façade and at the same time functions as a base for a beautiful cornice decorated with a freize of triglyphs and metopes.

On the recently-covered upper gallery, the Ionic columns and pilasters are arranged in a similar pattern to those on the lower floor. The upper columns, however, stand on a high guardrail.

The comparatively austere eastern façade of the Palace, can be seen from the **Partal** exit.

Work to the **Palace Chapel** was never completed nor were any decorative elements added. As mentioned previously, the Chapel stands in the northeastern corner of the Palace boasting an octagonal floor plan. The **Palace Crypt** is located underneath and currently opens out to the **Courtyard of the Myrtles** offering both enclosures a unique perspective of contrasting architectural styles. A plain cupola was recently added to the **Chapel** in order to protect it from the weather.

Galleries in inner courtyard.

THE SAINT MARY OF THE ALHAMBRA CHURCH

The building of this Church began on the site of the once splendid Great Mosque of the Alhambra, which was supposed to have been an outstanding example of its kind.

Work was said to have commenced on this Christian church in 1581, and finished in 1618; **Ambrosio de Vico** was the last architect to work on it.

Its ground plan is that of a latin cross, with side chapels. Its impressive, perfectly-gilded wood Baroque altarpiece is particularly outstanding. Attributed to Juan López de Almagro, this alterpiece, with its large wreathed columns, is dated from 1671. The two statue images of Saint Ursula with Susan, and the Crucifix respectively are the work of Alonso de Mena. The statue of the Virgen Mary, attributed to Torcuato Ruiz del Peral, is perhaps the best known since it is carried, on an embossed silver **throne** resembling the Courtyard of the Lion's arcade, through the streets of Granada in the Easter Week procession held on Holy Saturday.

View of Church tower from the Partal Gardens.

THE CHARLES V FOUNTAIN

The Charles V Fountain.

The **Charles V Fountain** is built into the Renaisance support wall near the **Gate of Justice.** Pilasters and rounded recesses with greatly deteriorated relief work decorate the wall. The fountain was designed by **Machuca** and is adorned with decorative designs sculpted by **Nicolás de Corte.** It has a pyramidal form at the base of which three masks represent the three

The Gate of the Pomegranates.

rivers of Granada: the **Genil, Darro** and **Beiro.** In the centre shields, symbols and a medallion with a dedication to the **Emperor** lie beneath the great imperial coat of arms that crowns the fountain, and the decorative figures of cherubs, snails and dolphins complete the design.

THE GATE OF THE POMEGRANATES

This further work by **Machuca** welcomes visitors to a new access to the Alhambra. Even its military simplicity has not escaped the pomegranates and angels that decorate it. Its bevelled ashlars, fashioned after the style of the Florentine palaces, and the grandeur of the central arch span, together with the two small side arches, are the features which most catch the vistor's attention.

Vase of the Gazelles.

MUSEUMS

THE NATIONAL HISPANO-ARAB ART MUSEUM

Objects found in the Alhambra, mainly resulting from chance findings or building works, have accumulated since the second half of the 19th century. Some of these have been exhibited in the Alhambra itself while others, often in fragments, were simply stored in a place that soon became known as the «El Museillo» or «Miniature Museum». Later they were classified and sorted, and in 1942 the Archeological Museum of the Alhambra was officially created and set up in the upper rooms of the Courtyard of the Myrtles. The Museum attained its present category as the National Hispano-Arab Art Museum on 13th December 1962.

The Alhambra Trust approved the construction of a building in the upper areas of Fuentepeña in 1967, and work commenced on 2nd January 1974, continuing until December 1975. Since then work has continued, with some alterations being made up to the present day.

The exhibition rooms of the Museum are chronologically ordered according to the characteristics of the exhibits.

The ceramic resources are the most numerous in the Museum, owing either to the characteristics of the medium or to the fact that the city attracted a large number of immigrants from elsewhere in Al-Andalus at the end of the period of Arab domination.

A caliphal plate is one of the most remarkable of the porcelain and ceramic assets, originally from the town of Medina Azahara as are other plates, bowls and domestic ware, many from the Nasrid period and some of considerable size.

But perhaps the Museum's most outstanding piece is the Gazelle Vase, made of Nasrid lustre-ware dating from the 14th century. The Simonetti Vase, from the collection of the same name, is a sister piece although of more modern design, and there are other noteworthy fragments of vases amongst which is the vase neck from Dr. Hirsch's collection.

The most remarkable of the tiled socles is the one originally from the Hall of the Aleyas in the Alhambra's Comares Palace that was later set in the Mexuar Courtyard. The Nasrid tiles from the Tower of the Queen's Dressing Room are undoubtedly the most important of the floor tiles. Some pieces of Fatimid ceramics acquired in Cairo are also worthy of mention.

The most outstanding in the wood section are pieces of inlaid work. In particular, a splendid cupboard of two large panels from the Granada Princes' Residence, a Nasrid mule-chair with an embossed leather back and a peculiar chess-board all dating from the 14th and 15th centuries. The 14th-century Nasrid wooden lattice window screen which originated in the Hall of the Two Sisters in the Courtyard of the Lions must also be mentioned. Various **mudéjar** suits of armour such as a 14th century suit from the Palace of the Merced in Granada are now exhibited in the new museum building, as are the pieces of 11th-century **mudéjar** eaves from Toledo and the Almohad and Protonasrid panels recently discovered in the Casa de los Tiros. Finally, the small Nasrid coffer with ivory inlay covering one of its sides is worthy of note.

The caliphal font from the Alamiriya Palace in Almanzor is another of the Museum's prized pieces and this is found in the marble section along with a 10th century

Socle originally from the Hall of the Aleyas, later used in the Mexuar.

caliphal base and capital, various Nasrid column bases, shafts and capitals from assorted origins, a number of finely worked gravestones from the Nasrid period and of special interest, an incomplete though perfectly recognisable sun dial. Last though not least is the 14th century foundation stone from Nasrid Maristan in the Albaicín, a building which was criminally demolished during the last century.

The most outstanding metal items are the 11th-century copper Yamur from the old Cadí mosque in Granada and assorted caliphal oil-lamps from various origins.

One of the most important pieces kept in the Museum is part of an oil-painted panel on gold backing, in which two Christian knights appear ready to attack, their two-

Marble caliphal font.

handed swords raised above their heads and a fortified city behind them. This item, recently restored, was miraculously preserved because it had been used in a previous roof repair. The Nasrid verse written in Spanish: «God is the only conqueror», which appears around the border, would lead us to believe that this repair was probably effected at the beginning of the 15th century by Christians.

From amongst numerous plaster friezes special mention must be made of those originally from the Acequia Lookout Tower in the Generalife, those from Arjona (Jaén), those from the Palace of the Alijares and the fragments from the Palace of the Bride on the Cerro del Sol hill.

Lastly we must also mention some Nasrid stone Maqabrlyyas as well as an assorted collection of stone fire-pans from various periods.

THE FINE ARTS MUSEUM

The Provincial Fine Arts Museum in housed on the upper floor of the Palace of Charles V. Work for its installation began in 1941 and was finalised in 1956. It was officially inaugurated in October 1958 to coincide with the 400th anniversary of the Emperor's death.

The Museum's collections were initially based on works contributed from the auction of legacies. These were progressively engrossed through acquisitions, deposits and donations until an outstanding collection, mainly centred on Granada's painting and sculpture dating from the 16th century to the mid-20th century.

The most remarkable of the early works are Roberto Aleman's Gothic Virgen which presided over the Gate of Justice, one of the entrances to the Alhambra, or those by Jacobo Florentino, or the wood embosses by Diego de Siloé, the rich Limoges enamel known as the Gran Capitán triple panel or the paintings by Pedro de Raxis.

One room is dedicated to the work of the Carthusian friar Juan Sánchez Cotán. His most outstanding painting is the famous Thistle Still Life, a work of mystic symbolism, of incomparable perfection and beauty. Another room is dedicated to the painter, sculptor and architect Alonso Cano and we can admire here the first two in the series called «Racionero» which is completed with the works by his closest disciples.

Fine Arts Museum.

Pedro de Mena, Anastasio Bocanegra and the 18th-century painters José Risueño, Chavarito and Torcuato Ruiz del Peral have some of their finest work in this Museum and these paintings are among the most outstanding.

Perhaps the most attractive room for the visitor is the Chimney Room. It is made of 16th-century Carrara marble which was especially ordered for the Palace, and decorated with rich tapestries, wall hangings and period furniture.

Of the 19th-century works, those of the Madrazo family, Emilio Sala, Moreno Carbonero and Pérez Villamil amongst others are worth noting.

The last room contains the work of Granada artists, mainly from the first half of the 20th century with paintings by Rodríguez-Acosta, López Mezquita and Gabriel Morcillo.

THE RICHES OF THE PRADO MUSEUM

On the left of the entrance hall to the Charles V Courtyard there is a small door which leads to a series of palace chambers which are used by the «Painting Museum» and where works which are part of the «riches of the Prado» are to be found. These works belong to this important museum although the Alhambra is under the obligation to protect and care for them while having the privilege of exhibiting them to visitors. There are paintings from different European schools and by (or at least attributed to) various universally-renowned painters.

THE ANGEL BARRIOS HOUSE-MUSEUM

Antonio Barrios, nicknamed the «Polinario», was a popular character in Granada who owned an inn on the Royal Avenue of the Alhambra which was frequented by both local and foreign intellectuals at the start of this century. Social gatherings, that Antonio Barrios accompanied with his guitar playing and singing, were held there. These meetings caused him to be awarded the honorary title of «Consul of Art in the Alhambra», the bestowal of which was witnessed by the signatures of Ravel and Strauss, amongst others.

Angel Barrios, son of the beloved «Polinario», brought up amid this cultural amalgam soon showed his artistic restlessness. He was musical; from an early age he played the violin, piano, guitar and he composed as well. He studied in Paris where he became friends with musicians such as Albéniz, Granados and Dukas. He formed part of the Iberia Trio as a guitarist and performed in France and England. He continued his studies in Madrid with Conrado del Campo.

He was a close friend of Manuel de Falla who became his daughter's god-father. In Barrios' house, so rich in sentimentalism and culture, gathered Eugenio D'Ors, Federico García Lorca, Zuloaga, Villaespesa, Rusiñol, Machado and a long ecetera of intellectuals and artists of a culturally flourishing period in Spain.

The Angel Barrios House-Museum, next to the Polinario Baths.

Angel Barrios was director of the Granada Music Conservatory, a member of the Fine Arts Academy of Our Lady of Anguish and Vice-Mayor on the town council of this city. He was the author of various compositions whose melodies evoke the very corners of the house. He died in Madrid on 26th November 1964 and his remains were transferred to Granada five years later.

The realization of this evocative Museum has been possible thanks to his childrens' donations fulfilling the musician's wishes. Inside one can contemplate side by side family memmentos, authentic works of art by the artists who once visited the house and the true passions of Barrios' life: his guitar and piano.

POLINARIO'S BATH

On the same Royal Avenue, next to the Angel Barrios House-Museum, there is a Arab bath which is called «Polinario's Bath» because it formed part of the famous inn. There is no doubt that it is the same one cited by Ibn al-Jatib as belonging to the Alhambra mosque and that both were built by Muhammad III for his own private use. The bath, hidden by the walls of a house built in either the 17th or 18th century, was restored and consequently studied after 1934.

The bath's internal distribution displays the common features that characterise this type of building. The base for the vaulting and the lantern as well as the pieces of tiling, plaster work, marble floors and basins gradually appeared from amongst the ruined remains so that today another building of the Arab Alhambra has been greatly recovered.

Due to the bath's similarity to the Royal Comares Bath, two main construction periods can be distinguished. The first being that of its founding and the second, some 30 or 50 years later, corresponds to an enlargement of the building, the lantern and probably some other annexes outside the bath itself.

TYPICAL SPOTS IN THE ALHAMBRA

THE ROYAL AVENUE

In Nasrid times, the Royal Avenue was the Alhambra's main artery, as it still is today. Public buildings, mansion-houses, residences, trading stalls and workshops used to stand along the main avenue's slightly sloping sides from its beginning at the Wine Gate to the easternmost end of the walled enclosure. Today the Avenue is hardly a third of its original length, having changed with the passing of the centuries. Nevertheless, it still preserves the living memory of its past with some houses, small souvenir shops, hotels and restaurants and even a handicraft workshop. It is the ideal place to stop during a visit to the Alhambra, rest, have a meal or buy a souvenir.

The Royal Avenue.

THE ARAB CISTERNS

In the middle of the Square of the Arab Cisterns stands a 19th century kiosk covering the curb of a working well that draws cool water from the Cisterns for those who ask for it, who should also try the typical **eau-de vie** meringue with it. This was a traditional meeting place for the citizens of Granada, the setting for **flamenco** festivals and frequented by such personalities as Manuel de Falla and Federico García Lorca. Today it has become almost a compulsory stopping place for a rest or refreshment.

Square of the Arab Cisterns.

THE POLINARIO

About halfway up the Royal Avenue stands the Polinario; once the site of the old inn belonging to Antonio Barrios, whose nickname has been given to the present-day premises. Here visitors may stop for a rest during their tour or perhaps have lunch in the modern restaurant that, nonetheless, preserves the flavour of Granada's traditions.

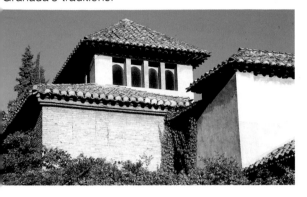

The Royal Avenue.

THE OSIER BED

At the exit from the Generalife is an area named after the trees that cover it —osiers; another ideal spot to rest and try traditional Granada cuisine. It is situated next to several craftsmen's houses which used to guard the entrance to the Generalife grounds. Still standing over the entrance gate is the coat of arms belonging to the Granada-Venegas Family, originally Arab converts to Christianity, and owners of the grounds.

La Mimbre Restaurant.

THE CARMEN DE LOS MARTIRES

The so-called **Campo de los Mártires** (or Field of the Martyrs), near the Alhambra, has one of the most characteristic «carmenes» (a typical Granada house with garden) in the city. Situated on the old Alhabul, at a place where numerous existing dungeons and silos were used to imprison Christians during Arab domination, some of whom were martyred according to tradition. The Catholic Monarchs, therefore, decreed the buildings of a hermitage under the denomination of the Martyred Saints.

At the end of the 16th century, the Carmen of the Martyrs was converted into a monastery for the Barefoot Carmelites, for which St. John of the Cross was a prior and in which he wrote most of his evocative poetic works. The friars of this Order made several alterations. The area which had been bare of vegetation until that time, was converted into a major wood and farming estate. This was worked by the friars until the Disentailment, when the monastery was demolished and its fields abandoned.

In 1845, Carlos de Calderón, bought the estate and built the large mansion-house that stands there today, and it was this Carlist General who was responsible for

Views of the Palace and Gardens.

the landscaping of the romanic gardens and lake.

In 1889 the poet Jòsé Zorrilla stayed at the Carmen. Two years later it was acquired by a Belgian, Humberto Mersmans, an important art collector, who embellished the Carmen where he would entertain important personalites and intellectuals from Granada, such as Manuel de Falla and Federico García Lorca.

In 1930, the Duke, Protector of the Princes, bought the Carmen though not taking charge of it until eight years later. It was declared a National Garden Monument in 1943. Four years later the Carmen was bequeathed to the Mother Superior of the Jerome Order, Sor Cristina de la Cruz Arteaga, who sold the grounds to Granada Town Hall in 1957.

At the beginning of the 1970's a large hotel was

planned, and work was even commenced, destroying a large portion of the century-old woods and ruining the gardens and mansion-house. Thanks to popular appeals, the project was brought to a halt, and the Town Hall began reinstating and restoring the Carmen, in collaboration with public and private institutions. Over the last ten years, one of the most beautiful spots in Granada has been recovered for posterity.

SHORT GUIDE OF GRANADA

Cathedral

The Catholic Monarchs decided in 1501 that the new Cathedral were built in the site of the former major mosque of the city.

Once the foundations laid and the front part built and after strong discussions between the Chapter and several social groups of influence in the city, it was decided that the burgeois artist, Diego de Siloe, defends his project in Renaissance style before the Emperor Carlos V, who approved it.

Siloe built a Cathedral with a big chancel covered by a dome and oppened with an ambulatory that allows walking between the five naves supported by corinthian columns with two smaller side-chapels. There are two doors on the North facade, the one giving to *De la Carcel* Street. The first one, called *Del Perdón*, is the most sumptuous one, the upper part carried out by Siloe and the lower part by Diego de Pesquera.

Alonso Cano designed in 1667 the main façade in a style far from Siloe´s project.

Royal Chapel

In 1504, the Catholic Monarchs left one of their best legacys for Granada when they decided to raise a chapel, a mausoleum for them, beside the Cathedral.

In 1506 the architect Enrique Egeas was put in charge of making the project. An austere and simple project for a masterpiece of Gothic architecture adjacent to the Cathedral. The Chapel ground-plan takes the shape of a Latin cross, complemented by a big choir on the upper floor. The façade, made around 1517, is a beautiful piece of flamboyant Gothic architecture. Inside the Chapel it is to point out: the impressing transept screen (*reja*) made by the masterly *Maestro* Bartolomé, regarded as one of the finest *rejas* in the world; the coffins of the Catholic Monarchs made in marble of Carrara by the Italian artist Fancelli and installed in 1520; and the coffins of Felipe the Fair and Juana the Mad entrusted by their son Carlos V to the Spanish sculptor Bartolomé Ordoñez. It is also to point out the impressing collection of Flemish paintings, dating from the XV century, donated by Queen Isabel.

Carthusian Monastery

It is the piece best representing the Baroque in Granada. It has its origin, as many other historic and religious foundations in Granada, in the arrival of the Catholic Monarchs in 1492 and the ascetic and mystic religiosity of the Carthusian monks. The cloister, a simple court sorrounded by a series of arcades supported by doric columns, is oppened to a garden with a fountain in the middle. In the adjacent rooms, with beautiful vaults with ribs, the lay monk, Juan Sánchez Cotán, drew a true chronical of the monastic order. Together with Cotán´s there are other oil paintings of Vicente Cartucho. The Church of a sole nave, in which we can find several paintings of Pedro Anastasio Bocanegra about the life of the Virgin, is divided in three areas: the front part, for the faithful; in the middle, the choir for the laity; and the rest for the Carthusian monks. The Tabernacle has the symbolism of being the first cell of the Monastery for Jesus Christ, symbol, according to the peculiar way of life of the Carthusians, of both the life in common and the lonelyness.

San Jeronimo's Monastery

San Jerónimo´s Monastery and Church are a key piece in the urban organization of the Catholic Monarchs after the Conquest. Later on it would be a focal point of the urban development when the Emperor ceded the Chancel of the Church to María Manrique, widow of the *Gran Capitán* and duchess of Sessa, as a burial place for them and their descendants. The Widow moved with her family and vassals, from 1513 to 1525, to a near palace, creating a new quarter with the name of *Duquesa* (Duchess). About the Monastery, it is Known that the big cloister was finished in 1519, and the second one a year later. About this second cloister, where the Empress Isabel lived when she visited Granada during her honey moon, the Ambassador Navagiero said "it has gardens, fountains and two beautiful cloisters never seen before, but the new one, with orange trees and other plants in the middle, is bigger and more magnificient than the other". The Duchess commended the Church, with a strong Renaissance personality, from 1528 on, to Diego de Siloe.

Corral del Carbón

Arab caravanserai, also known as *Al-yadida* or the new one. This building was at the same time a store building and a lodging for merchants. The store and stables on the ground floor and the rooms for guests on the first and second floor. A bridge called *Qantarat Al-yadida* connected it with the cultural, commercial and religious centre at that time. Built around the XIV century, it is the only caravanserai still preserved in Spain. The building has only one entry that is outwardly decorated, something not very usual in the Hispanic- Moslem art. On the facade there is a horseshoe arch made of brick with sculpted festoons on the archivolt limiting the triangular space formed by the *albanegas* covered with *Ataurique* decoration sculpted in plaster. Over the moulding, limiting the *alfiz*, there is epigraphic decoration in *Cúfico*. On the second wing, just in the middle, there is a *twin* window. The vestibule is covered by a vault with plaster *Mocárabes* stalactites probably polichromatic in their origin. At both sides, false decorative arches made of plaster and at the back an architraved door with false dovetails of the same material.

The *Madraza* Palace

The *Madraza* is for the Moslem like the University for us. It was finished in 1349 by Yusuf I on the initiative of his Prime Minister, Ridwan. It was built in front of the mosque *Aljama*, and was entirely conservated until the XVI century, and for its most part until almost the end of the XVIII century. It was made imitating the most famous schools of the other side of the Straits of Gibraltar and against Andalucian learning traditions, despite the previous existence of other schools in Málaga and Murcia. The building was opened to the Major Mosque´s Square, now the market square between the Madraza and the Royal Chapel. The Catholic Monarchs transferred this building to the city in order that it were the Town Council seat. That in the XIX century would move to the former convent in the Square *del Carmen*. In this century the *Madraza*, that moved to private hands, lost its roof and *Mocárabes* stalactites in a fire from which only survived the alicer. It was restored in 1893 by Mauricio Contreras, architect in charge of preserving the Alhambra. In 1860 the only part dating from Moslem times still preserved, the *Mihrab* of the oratory, was discovered.

Realejo

The *Realejo* is one of the oldest quarters in Granada. It had two outskirts, the High *Realejo* and the Low *Realejo*. Inhabitted mainly by weavers, it brings together a melting pot of the tree cultures: the Jewish, the Moslem and the Christian, something determinant for the development of this quarter. The Jewish minority inhabitting the Realejo welcomed the Islamic invaders with open hands because they liberated them from the Visigothic joke. Starting there a long period of pacific convivence, until the end of the Ziri Dynasty, when they almost disappeared. During the Moslem occupation, the quarter, plenty of *Cármenes*, vegetable gardens and irrigation ditchs, was characterized by the contact with nature. The Christian Conquest meant a radical change in the appearance of the quarter. In 1497, on the occasion of the celebration of the wedding of Prince Juan and Princess Margarita of Austria part of the quarter was flattened, hence the name given to the resulting place, *Campo del Príncipe*. San Cecilio´s, patron saint of the city, Parish Church was founded, as it happened with most of the Catholic churchs, in 1501 in the site of a former mosque.

Sacromonte

Stretched along a semideserted hill and dipping down its slode lies the *Sacromonte*, a little mysterious quarter formed of subterranean caves, once inhabited by gypsies, connected by paths and lanes flanked by agaves and prickly pears. Nowdays the quarter inhabited by gypsies has almost disappear. Now the caves are bars and *Zambras* (typical gipsy dance). If you go on you will come accross another mount named *Valparaíso*, on the top of which we find the Sacromonte Abbey and *San Cecilio* Collegiate Church. This last one ordered to be built by the Archbishop Pedro de Castro at the beginning of the XVII century, because two treasure prospectors found there, in 1594, human remains of the martyrs San Cecilio, San Tesifón and San Hiscio, later named patron saints of Granada. Several leaden sheets supposed to belong to the famous leaden books were also found that, though at the beginnig deceived even Felipe II, resulted to be a forgery.

Royal Hospital

It was founded by the Catholic Monarchs in 1504 to attend the needs of the poor people and the pilgrims. It was designed by the architect Enrique Egeas and its construction begun in 1511. But the work stopped in 1516 due to the death of the King until 1522, when his grandson Carlos V renewed it. The second floor was raised in 1527 and the facade was finished in the XVII century. Until not long ago the Royal Hospital lodged people of the province of Granada suffering from mental illness. The Hospital has experienced many changes in its 500 years of life due to the slowness of the work and to fashion aesthetic changes. Because of this it has elements of the Gothic, beginning of the Renaissance and Baroque. Nowdays it is the seat of the Rectorship of the University of Granada and the Library, with around one thousand books and the general card index for all the libraries of the University.

San Juan de Dios Hospital

It was openned in *San Jerónimo* Street, its site at the moment, in 1552, built with the contributions of the Widow of the *Gran Capitán* and other important people like Diego de Siloe, who left his possessions to the Hospital. Beside the Hospital there is *San Juan de Dios* Church, finished in 1759. The facade is fitted between two high towers of stone crowned by spires covered with slate. The ground-plan takes the shape of a Latin cross with four chapels openned in the walls of its sole nave. The Church, built and decorated in no more than two decades by the same constructor, is of a magnificent richness. The Church has several side-chapels, an important collection of sculptures and paintings dating from the XVII and XVIII century. Beside the Church there is *San Rafael* Old People's Home and Hospital built in the last third of the XIX century and rebuilt in the last decade of the XX century. It also receives orphan children and has a children hospital.

Arch *de Elvira*

Also Known as Door *de Elvira* or *Bib-Elvira*, is so named because it was the beginning of the route to the city of Elvira and because, due to its importance and size it was the main door of Granada. Different sources, both Christian and Islamic, have talked about it since the XIII century. The work was started in the middle of the XI century reigning Ziri de Habus. What nowdays still stands up belongs to the part transformated during the XIV century, *nazarí* period. It is basically a horseshoe arch giving to an open court. Close to the Door *de Elvira* have been found remains of an ancient Moorish bath Known as the *Casa de las tumbas*, domolished at the beginning of the XX century. Outside the Arch of Elvira was the Moslem cemetery of the city, whose remains have been found in the Square *del Triunfo*, in the work of the Royal Hospital, at the beginning of the Avenue *de la Constitución* and in the former School of *Magisterio*.

Santa Ana's Church

Built in the place of the little mosque of the *Almanzora* quarter, founded by the king Ziri Badis, it was set up as parish church in 1501 and built in 1537 by Diego de Siloe. The tower is made of brick, as the rest of the church, it has balconys with arches and triangular *albanegas* with white and blue ornamental tiles that can also be seen in the cornice and the spire. Inside the Church, the central chapel has a magnificent *mudejar* frame work with knot figures. The black humanist Juan Latino was buried in this church, as well as the painter and sculptor Juan Risueño and the historian Francisco Bermudez Pedraza. There got married the liberal heroine Mariana Pineda. Opposite the church and joining the right border of the river Darro with the *Almanzora* quarter there was a bridge made of stone called *del Cadi*. It disappeared when arching the river and extending the Square *Nueva* by lowering the level of the ground, what resulted in the elevation of the Church on a modern outside staircase.

Santo Domingo's Church

Part of the *Huerta* (vegetable garden) *del Cuarto Real* and hence of the *Santa Cruz* Monastery. It started to be built in 1512 and its work, masonry and decoration are of Renaissance style. Its facade is a portico with tree round arches supported by doric coumns in whose triangular *albanegas* appear the initials of the Catholic Monarchs and the motto "*Tanto monta monta tanto*" (relating to the fact that both Isabel and Fernando governed with the same power). The ground-plan takes the shape of a Latin cross, with five chapels in each of its sides covered by vaults with ribs. The transept experienced modifications at the end of the XVII century when it was decided to build the side-chapel of the Rosario Virgin. In the middle of the altar piece you can see a sculpture of the Rosario Virgin dating from the XVII century, which wear a siverplated dress adorned with colourful precious stones. Here is where the Inquisition Tribunal celebrated its festivities, and in its chapels is where the members of the most influencing families of Granada, as the Varela or the Girones were burried.

Square del Carmen

During the XIX century and as a consequence of the secularization started in 1836, emerged in the city centre new public places occupying the sites of disentailed convents. Among the clearest examples are the Square *de la Trinidad* and the Convent *del Carmen*, now the Square *del Carmen* and the main building of he Twon Council. Gallego Burin called this last square "the square of the politics or the politicians". As the people from Granada only go there for administrative reasons or when the mayoralty call them for the conmemoration of the taking of the city by the Catholic Monarchs, *Toma*, (that in the last occasions has provoque confrontations with the Andalucian Nationalist Party), for the Day *de la* Cruz (in which a cross of flowers and a portable bar are placed in front of the Twon Council building), for the festivities of the *Corpus Christi* with its sideshow of *Feria* and for New Year´s Eve, to eat the traditional grapes with the sound of the peals of the Twon Council Clock´s bells. Until no long the aesthetic and the volume of the buildings around the Twon Council did not contrast with its facade.

Bib-Rambla Square

It has always been the heart of the city. In Moslem times this square was beside the *Arenal del Rio*, hence its name. There took place, as the last king Ziri reports in first person in his book dating from the XI century, jousts and festivities.

At the begining of the XVI century the square would be extended by building arcades. The square played an important role during the *Corpus Christi* festivities instituted by the Catholic Monarchs. The importance taken by this festivities pushed the Twon Council towards the building of a house from where to see the events. Diego de Siloe was charged of the design of the building whose structure would be part of the Arch *de las Orejas*. It was destroyed by a fire the 31st of December 1879. The catastrophe took place again at New Yaer´s Eve 1982, destroying the *Curia* as well as the Achbishop´s Palace, still to be rebuilt. The fountain in the middle of the square, called *De los Gigantones*, belonged to the ancient *San Agustin´s* Convent.

Park of Ciences

The Park of ciences is an interactive museum in the line of the most avanced European centres. There the visitors have the opportunity of enjoying with the world of cience and environment, astronomy and human beings, all this in an active and amusing way. The main building is placed in a spacious precinct of 30,000 m2, a modern equipment with the last technologies in which you will find 6 rooms of permanent exposition and 2 of temporal expositions, a planetarium with capacity for 83 people, assembly room, cafeteria and a spacious glazed hall with a Foucault pendulum of 12 m. Outside, there are an astronomic observatory, a tropical butterfly sanctuarium, interactive games with water, botany experiments, a tent for celebrations, an oil press, a vegetal labirynth and other areas of different thematic content. Within its future projects it is to point out the Pavilion for Temporal Expositions, the Andalician Centre of Environment, an Observation and Telecomunication Tower 30 m. high, a lake and a restaurant with intelligent technologies applied to nourishment and nutrition.

Nuestra Señora de las Angustias Church

It had its origin in a little hermitage, until in 1567 Felipe II ceded a site for the construction of a hospital and in 1664 a church was built in part of this plot. It would be the Parish Church *Nuestra Señora de las Angustias*, patron saint of the city, what increases the ritual value of this area, *Carrera de la Virgen*, a parade for the people from Granada, thanks to the processions and visits to the Virgin.

The façade is flanked by two high towers, built in the XVIII century, crowned by spires covered with glazed tiles. The façade is corinthian, made of stone of *Sierra Elvira*, with salomonic columns, inside which there are sculptures of the Virgin *de las Angustias*, crowned with the real shield.

Inside the church there is the side chapel of the Virgin, Where the devotion of the people from Granada reaches its zenith. It is decorated with all the Baroque splendour and, at the same time, is one of the first pieces of the *Churrigeresco* style.

Casa de los Tiros

This house is named *Casa de los tiros* because of the muskets appearing on the top of its façade. The building was built over what were the fortified city walls. The first information about this house dates from 1510, in 1530 it moved to the hands of the Granada Venegas family, descendants of the *Nazari* real family, who started to built the house we can see nowdays. From outside, it has the shape of a tower. The battlements almost disappeared when, recently, a modern roof was added.

There are two balconys in the façade as well as overhanging brackets with five sculptures. In the middle of the transept there is a sculpted sword with his sharp end touching a heart, at which cides there is the following inscription "*El Manda*".

Inside the palace there is a spacious vestibule covered with magnificient batten.

Nowdays there is a newspaper archive and a library versing on Granada, and a museum, whose finality is to recover the atmosphere that surrounded the landmarks in Granada´s history.

The *Albaicín*

The origin of this quarter dates from the Iberian and Roman occupation , but it is not until the VIII century that a fortress called *His-garnata* was started to be built, on the top of the hill, in the place of the former square *de San Nicolás*, called Citadel *Cadima* or old during the *Ziri* dynasty times. In the XI century a village settlement emerged around the citadel, which started to be called the suburb of the *Albaicín*. It is there where the *Ziri* dynasty stablished its court. But the Almoravids or Almohads governors kept on governing the city from the citadel *Cadima*. *During the* Ziri dynasty times, the quarter had its *Alhama* (major) mosque, what nowdays is the Church *de San Salvador*, several Moorish baths, a great number of cisterns, its own justice administration and its *Maristan* (hospital), built by the *Nazari* king Muhamad V.

Nowdays the *Albaicín* is much bigger than the little suburb it was in Moslem times. What nowdays is known as the *Albaicín* accomplish many Moslem quarters constituting one of the biggest *medina* still preserved in our days.

Conventions Palace

Granada has a new and beautiful palace, the Expositions and Conventions Palace. It is placed in its urban heart, the best possible place, with easy access for everybody.

Granada has equiped its Expositions and Conventions Palace with the most advanced technology and has designed it to be versatile and able to welcome, with the same efectivity and enthousiasm, all kind of meeting, it does not matter if it is the presentation of a product, a convention or commercial exposition, a concert or a company convention.

TOURIST ROUTES IN THE PROVINCE

Sierra Nevada Mountains

To visit Sierra Nevada Mountains means to enjoy adventure, snow and ski. There, you are sorounded by lagoons and little Mediterranean forests. You discover a Nature Park, a Biosphere Reserve and a National Reserve for Hunting, in which you can find more than 60 botanic species exclusive from this region and a rich fauna from which it is to point out the wild goat.

It means to contemplate an incredibly beautiful landscape, that extends to most of the south of Spain, The Mediterranean sea and even a horizon limited by the African coast.

And all this, near the sky, from the highest massif in occcidental Europe, with a high above sea level higher than (3,000) metres From the Mulhacen peak (3,481 m.), roof of the Iberian Peninsula, or the Veleta peak (3,470 m.) protecting the ski runs which go down its slode.

Guadix and *Marquesado* de Zenete

This extended plain shows us the contrasts and earth reddish colours of *Marquesado* de Zenete. Lines of almond trees, beautiful when flowered, lead us to big extensions of dry land crossed by herds of sheeps and goats which graze quietly. Dawns of hoarfrost and warm dusks after hot days offer us the few shadows that extend along the plains, the shadows of La Calahorra castle-palace that, from the top of the hill, visually dominates the *Marquesado*, the shadows of the *mudejar* church towers of its white villages, the shadows of the *Alcazar* (ancient Moslem citadel) and the Cathedral of Guadix which go down to the troglodyte caves quarter in which white chimneys emerge from the earth. A place where time does not passes, where the quiet lifes of its people take place at the foot of Sierra Nevada Mountains.

Alpujarra

Country of nowhere. In Garcia Lorca´s words these lands can be summarize in three words: folklore, popular festivities and superstition.

Villages that, immersed in an ancient time, show us their liveness and hapiness. And they do it through narrow Moslem streets hanging from the slodes of the mountains, with whitewashed walls, streets made of wood, balconys, geraniums and smoky chimneys which break the horizon of the snow-capped Sierra Nevada Mountains, as well as the green of the landscape and the blue of the Mediterranean sea which, to the south, reaches the coast of Granada. Villages of mystery, that show at or hide from the fertile valley of the river Guadalfeo, the ravines and streams which inundate the landscape among vineyards, almond trees and fig trees.

Time stops, scents ride the winds and brush-strokes of colour splash the landscape. Sounds of singing and dancing come to us from the bottom of the valley: *Trovo, Taranto, Robao* or *Música de Ánimas. Fiesta de Moros y Cristianos* (festivities of Moorish and Christians) that get together the pieces of an ancient culture heritage.

Baza and Plateau

A long path of 100 kilometres among lunar lands, hard and dry, is what we find in this plateau, placed at 1,000 metres, reminiscence of the inmense lake that occupied these lands millions of years ago.

An enormous stepped crossed by the lines of green rivers that water the litle rich lowland areas emerging like oasis beside the villages tha mark this fascinating plain. Lordly villages, full of history, archaeological sites, caves that have been traditional houses for centurys and now are in fashion as part of rural tourism.

West of Granada

In the west of Granada we find, at each step, fountains, coats of arms, bridges and towers which remind us that these lands were the enclave of the last *Andalusi* frontier.

A rich history-art heritage, result of the intersection of routes and cultures. From the important archaeological sites to the remains of the Iberian, Roman or Visigothic civilizations, and mainly the Arabs legacy.

Nature, history and the urban-rural balance make the west of Granada one of the main exponents of inner Andalucia.

Villages founded on flat hills, cuts and *sierras*. In their streets we find history; in their people kindness, costumes and traditions.

Tropical Coast

When we reach the south, the Tropical Coast, we find infinite reasons to be happy. All is light, sun, sea and warm temperatures during all the year.

We embrace the sea among steep white streets of beautiful villages that rise to the sky, contemplating the horizon, like in other times, Phoenicians, Romans and Arabs did.

We feel the protection of the imposing Sierra Nevada Mountains over this steep and beautiful lands. Bananas, avocados and custard apples constitute its exotic subtropical vegetation. Work of sugar cane and millennial salt of people with kind eyes that invite us to remain in this place of quietness and rest.

A land of warm summers and cool winters, looking to the sea, that urge you to enjoy your leisure time, to go swimming, practice sports and spend warm pleasant nights.

Hotels

Hotels (****)   Telf.

P.N. San Francisco. Alhambra 958 221440/41
Alhambra Palace. Peña Partida, 2 .... 958 221468
Carmen. Acera del Darro, 62 .... 958 258300
Meliá Granada. Angel Ganivet, 7 .... 958 227400
Princesa Ana. Avda. Constitución, 37 .... 958 287447
Rallye. Paseo de Ronda, 107 .... 958 272800
Triunfo Granada. Plª del Triunfo, 19 .... 958 207444
Saray. Tierno Galván s/n 958 130009
Granada Center. Avda. Fuente Nueva s/n ... 958 205000
Tryp Albayzín. Carrera del Genil, 48 .... 958 220002
San Antón. Prolongación de San Antón 958 520100

Hotels (***)

Aben Humeya. Avda. de Madrid, 10 .... 958 295061
Los Alixares. Avda. Alixares del Generalife, s/n 958 225506
Anacapri. Joaquín Costa, 7 .... 958 227477/76
Ana María. Camino de Ronda, 101 .... 958 289215
Los Angeles. Cuesta Escoriaza, 17 .... 958 221424
Cóndor. Avda. Constitución, 6 .... 958 283711
Dauro. Acera del Darro, 19 .... 958 222150
Dauro II. Navas, 5 .... 958 221581
Gran Vía Granada. Postigo de Velutti s/n 958 285464
Guadalupe. Avda. de los Alixares s/n 958 223423
Inglaterra. Cetti-Marien 958 221558
Juan Miguel. Acera del Darro, 24 .... 958 521111
Reino de Granada. Recogidas, 53 .... 958 265878
San Gabriel. Ctra. Murcia, Km. 279 .... 958 201211
Washington Irving. Paseo del Generalife, 2 .... 958 227550

Hotels (**)

Don Juan. Martínez de la Rosa, 9 .... 958 285811
Macía. Plaza Nueva, 4 .... 958 227535
Montecarlo. Acera del Darro, 44 .... 958 257900
Presidente. Recogidas, 11 .... 958 253612/16
Reina Ana María. Sócrates s/n 958 209861
Sacromonte. Plaza del Lino, 1 .... 958 266411
Sierra Nevada. Avda. de Madrid, 74 .... 958 150951
Los Tilos. Plaza de Bib-Rambla, 4 .... 958 266712
Universal. Recogidas, 16 .... 958 260010
Los Jerónimos. Gran Capitán, 1 .... 958 294461

Hotels (*)

América. Real de la Alhambra, 53 .... 958 22747
Carlos V. Plaza Los Campos, 4 .... 958 22158
Niza. Navas, 16 .... 958 225430
Britz. Cuesta Gomerez, nº 1 .... 958 223652
H. R. Lisboa. Plaza del Carmen 958 221414

Hotels a las afueras de Granada

Príncipe Felipe. (Albolote) 958 46541
Alcano Sol. Ctra. de Málaga, Km. 437 .... 958 283050
Los Galanes. Ctra. Bailén -Motril, Km. 436 .. 958 570511
Kenia Granada. Sierra Nevada 958 48091
Las Terrazas (Bubión) 958 763034
Hostal Mirador de Loja 958 320041
Balneario Alhama de Granada 958 350011
Helios. (Almuñécar) 958 63445
Hotel San Marcos. (Mecina Fondales) 958 766131
Hotel Perla de Andalucía. Carchuna 958 62424
Hostal El Ciervo. (Sierra Nevada) 958 48046

Restaurants

Telf.

Tendido 1, (Plaza de Toros). Dr. Olóriz 958 272302
Mirador de Morayma. Albayzín. 958 228290
Cunini. Plaza Pescadería, 14 .... 958 250777
Chikito. Plaza del Campillo, 9 .... 958 223364
Horno de Santiago. Plaza de los Campos, 8 ..... 958 223476
Puerta Elvira. (Hotel Triunfo-Granada) 958 207444
Rincón de Miguel. Avda. Andaluces, 2 .... 958 292978

Sevilla. C/ Oficios, nº 12 .... 958 221223
Las Tinajas. C/ Martínez Campos, 17 .... 958 254393
Velázquez. C/ Emilio Orozco, 1 (detrás Edif. Americano) 958 280109
Tavares. Carrera del Genil, 4 .... 958 226769
Colombia. C/ Antequeruela Baja, s/n 958 227433
Pizzería Altamura. Avda. Andaluces, 2 .... 958 272908
Alcaicería. C/ Oficios, 6 .... 958 224341
Kudamm 1. Pedro Antonio de Alarcón, 43 .... 958 251718
La Gaviota. Avda. Andaluces, ? 958 292572
Pilar del Toro. Hospital de Santa Ana, 12 .... 958 225470
El Diván del Tamarit. Escudo del Carmen, 2 .... 958 223000
Las Tomasas. Carril de San Agustín (Albayzín) 958 224108
Pepe Toro. Carmino de Ronda, 101 .... 958 279865
Rincón de la Virgen. Ancha de la Virgen, 4 .... 958 221039
La Corrala del Carbón. Mariana Pineda, 8 .... 958 223810
Gallio. Plaza Bib-Rambla, 8 .... 958 221015
China. Pedro Antonio de Alarcón, 23 .... 958 250200
Real Asador de Castilla. Escudo del Carmen, 17 .... 958 222910
La Pesquería. Capuchinas, 14 (Plaza de la Romanilla) 958 521555
Manolo. Plaza Bib-Rambla 958 262070

RESTAURANTS CERCANOS A GRANADA

La Cabaña. Campo de Golf (Las Gabias) 958 584060
Venta de Riofrío. Ctra. Granada-Málaga, Km. 97 .... 958 321066
El Cortijo (Hotel Bobadilla). 958 321861
Ruta del Veleta. C/ Ctra. Sierra Nevada, 50 .... 958 486134
Tropical/Motril. Rodríguez Acosta, 23 .... 958 600450
El Palacio del Capricho. C/ Granada (Monachil) 958 500057
Horno de Víznar. Avda. Andalucía, nº 2 .... 958 540253
Aguas Blancas. Carretera del Pantano de Quéntar 958 485295

RESTAURANTS CERCANOS A LA ALHAMBRA

Jardines Alberto (Frente Generalite) 950 224818
La Mimbre (Bosques de la Alhambra) 958 222276
Colombia. Antequeruela Baja, 1 .... 958 227433

105

Salas Rocieras and *Zambra*

Telf.

Los Tarantos. El Sacromonte, 9 .... 958 22 45 25

Jardines Neptuno. Arabial, s/n 958 52 25 33

Reina Mora. Carretera de Murcia 958 40 12 65

Cueva María La Canastera. Sacromonte 958 67 10 22

Cueva El Rocío. Camino del Sacromonte, 70 ...... 958 22 71 29

Los Canasteros. Carril de San Cecilio, s/n 958 22 11 00

DISCOTHÈQUES

Granada 10. C/ Cárcel Baja, 10 .... 958 22 66 40

Perkusión. Plaza de Gracia, 9 .... 958 25 29 96

Ya. C/ Santa Bárbara 958 29 57 63

Distrito 10. Gran Capitán, 5 .... 958 28 02 90

Kripta. (Años 60. Música y Parejas). C/ Gran Capitán, 25 .... 958 29 37 98

Palacio de la Música. Arabial, 162 .... 958 27 74 21

Camping

GRANADA

Camping Motel Sierra Nevada 958 15 00 62

ALPUJARRA

Balcón de Pitres (Pitres) 958 76 61 11

COAST

El Paraíso (Almuñécar) 958 63 23 70

El Cortijo (Castell de Ferro) 958 65 60 83

Don Cactus (Motril) 958 62 31 09

Tapeo around Granada

FISHIES AND SEAFOOD
Cunini. Plaza Pescadería, 14
Rincón Taurino. C/ Sarabias, 5
Bar David. San Miguel Alta, 35
Casa Ramón. Camino de Ronda, 81
Restaurante La Gaviota. Avda. Andalucía, 2
El Gallo Rojo. Ctra. Málaga, Km.5

Zarza Mora. Camino de Ronda, 98
La Curva. Paseo de Colón, 38 (Albolote)
La Esquinita. Campo del Príncipe.
La Pesquería. Capuchinos, 14

SAUSAGES AND WINE
Taberna de Enrique "El Elefante". Puerta Real
Leo. C/ Sarabia, 3
Taberna "El Ajolí". Plaza Mariana Pineda
La Trastienda. Plaza Nueva
Chikito. Plaza Campillo, 9
Tendido 1. (Plaza Toros). Dr. Olóriz
Mesón Gregorio. Paseo Basilios, 5.
Rincón de la Virgen. Ancha de la Virgen, 4

Useful telephone numbers

POLICIA NACIONAL 091
POLICIA MUNICIPAL 092
BOMBEROS 958 203222 (080)
CRUZ ROJA (INFORMACION) 958 222166
GUARDIA CIVIL 958 251100 (062)
SEGURIDAD SOCIAL 958 282000
INF. TOXICOLOGIA 91 2620420
TELEGRAMAS POR TELEFONO 958 222000
RENFE .... 958 271272 - 958 223119
ESTACION DE AUTOBUSES 958 185480
AEROPUERTO DE GRANADA 958 447081
AYUDA EN CARRETERA 91/7421213
TELE RUTA (Estado carretera) 91/4417222
HOSPITAL CLINICO. Avda. de Madrid 958 807000
CORREOS. Puert a Real 958 224835
TELE-TAXI 958 280654
RADIO-TAXI 958 132323
AYUNTAMIENTO. Plaza del Carmen 958 248100
PATRONATO PROVINCIAL DE TURISMO 958 223527/28
OFICINA DE TURISMO (Mariana Pineda) 958 226688
CETURSA (Sierra Nevada) 958 249100
ESTACION DE ESQUI (Información Permanente) 958 249119
AMBULANCIA Y FUNERARIA 958 272130
IBERIA-AVIACO (Líneas Aéreas) 958 227592
ASOCIACION DE GUIAS DE GRANADA 958 229936
PROTECCION CIVIL 958 278650
DELEGACION DE CONGRESOS 958 246825
ALBERGUE CARRETERA 958 480405
FERIA DE MUESTRAS (IFAGRA) 958 810311
SERVICIOS MEDICOS-A.T.S. (24 horas) 958 255358/59
PALACIO DE CONGRESOS 958 246700
CAMBIO DE MONEDA
AMERICAN EXPRESS. Reyes Católicos 958 224512
CHEQUE POINT. Reyes Católicos 958 210592
HOTELES 4 ESTRELLAS/AGENCIAS DE VIAJES
BANCO DE GRANADA. C/ Gran Vía, 16 .... 958 225561
CAJA DE AHORROS DE GRANADA. Plª. Villamena, 1 .... 958 271399
BANCO DE VIZCAYA. Pl.ª del Carmen, 3 .... 958 225410
CENTROS QUE GARANTIZAN ACTIVIDADES CULTURALES
NEGOCIADO CULTURAL DEL AYUNTAMIENTO DE GRANADA
C/ Cuesta Santa Inés, 6 .... 958 229344
AREA DE CULTURA DE LA DIPUTACION PROVINCIAL
Palacio de los Condes de Gabia, 1 .... 958 255811
AUDITORIO MANUEL DE FALLA. Campo de los Mártires, s/n 958 227339
IGLESIA DE DIVERSAS CONFESIONES
IGLESIA EVANGELISTA. Callejón del Pretorio, s/n. 958 122306
IGLESIA ESPAÑOLA BAUTISTA. C/ Angel Barrios, 10 .... 958 261460
BALNEARIOS DE LA PROVINCIA DE GRANADA
ALHAMA DE GRANADA. Avda. del Balnearios, s/n. 958 350011
ALICUN DE LAS TORRES. Carretera de Gorafe, s/n 958 694022
LANJARON. Avda. del Generalísimo, 50 .... 958 771070
CAMPING
SIERRA NEVADA 1.ª CATEGORIA. Ctra. de Jaén, 107 .... 958 150062
ALQUILER DE COCHES
AUTOS FORTUNA. C/ Infanta Beatriz, 2 .... 958 260254
AI QUIAUTO, Rent a Car. C/ Beethoven, s.n 958 135750
AGENCIA DE VIAJES
VIAJES BONAL. María Luisa de Dios, 1 .... 958 276312
VIAJES SACROMONTE. Angel Ganivet, 6 .... 958 225598
EXCURSIONES
GRANAVISION. C/ Beethoven s/n, Nave 3, 1ª Planta 958 135804
CAMPO DE GOLF LOS CORSARIOS. Las Gabias 958 584477
CLUB DE GOLF LOS MORISCOS. Motril 958 825527
ALSINA GRAELLS. (Viajes diarios a Madrid). Ctra de Jaén, s/n 958 185480

Timetable of the main monuments and museums

MONUMENTOS	TELF.	DIAS DE VISITA	HORARIO
Alhambra y Generalife	958 220912	Lunes a Domingo	08,30 a 20,00 h.
Entrada restringida a 8.800 personas diarias			
Visita nocturna		Mart., Juev. y Sàb.	22,00 a 00,00 h.
Venta anticipada en cualquier sucursal del Banco Bilbao Vizcaya			
Venta telefónica: 902 224 460			

RESERVAS: Fax 958 21 05 84 Telf. 958 227532
Concertación previa a través de Agencias de Viaje, Guías, Hoteles.

Entrada 1.000 Ptas. Gratuitos menores de 8 años. Mayores de 65 años documentados de l
Comunidad Europea 375 ptas. Minusválidos y centros de enseñanza con concertación previa, los grupo
deben reservar en el siguiente número de teléfono: 958 22 09 12.

Nota: 15 minutos antes de la hora de cierre se efectuará el desalojo de los recintos. (La entrada
en vigor de los horarios se hace en función al cambio de hora).

* Para los visitantes nocturnos recoger los billetes en los primeros 45 minutos.

MONUMENTOS	TELF.	DIAS DE VISITA	HORARIO
Catedral (Entrada por Gran Vía)	958 222959	Mañanas	10,30 a 13,30 h.
		Tardes	16,00 a 19,00 h.
		Domingos	16,00 a 19,00 h.
Capilla Real (Entrada por C/ Oficios)	958 229239	Mañanas	10,30 a 13,00 h.
		Domingos y Festivos	11,00 a 13,00 h.
		Tardes	16,00 a 19,00 h.
Monasterio Cartuja (Real de la Cartuja)	958 161932	Mañanas	10,00 a 13,00 h.
		Domingo	10,00 a 12,00 h.
		Tardes	16,00 a 19,00 h.
Monasterio de S. Jeónimo	958 279337	Mañanas	10,00 a 13,00 h.
		Tardes	16,00 a 19,00 h.
Corral del Carbón	958 225990	Lunes a Sábado	9,00 a 19,00 h.
		Domingo	10,00 a 14,00 h.
El Bañuelo	958 222339	Martes a Sábado	10,00 a 14,00 h.
		Festivos cerrado	
Colegiata del Salvador	958 278644	Mañanas	10,30 a 13,00 h.
		Tardes	16,30 a 18,30 h.
		Domingo cerrado	
Museo Max Moreau	958 293310	Martes a Sábado	10,00 a 13,30 h.
		Festivos cerrado	16,00 a 18,00 h.
Basílica de San Juan de Dios	958 275700	Mañanas	7,30 a 10,30 h.
		Tardes	18,00 a 21,00 h.
Carmen de los Mártires	958 227953	Mañanas	10,00 a 14,00 h
		Tardes	17,00 a 19,00 h
		Sáb., Dom. y festiv.	10,00 a 19,00 h
Huerta de San Vicente Museo García Lorca Visitas guiadas cada 30 minutos	958 258466	Mañanas	10,00 a 13,00 h
		Tardes	17,00 a 20,00 h
		Lunes cerrado	
Abadía del Sacromonte Visitas guiadas cada 30 minutos	958 221445	Mañanas	11,00 a 13,00 h
		Tardes	16,00 a 18,00 h
		Lunes cerrado	
Museo Arqueológico	958 225640	Martes	15,00 a 20,00 h
		Miércoles a Sáb.	9,00 a 20,00 h
		Domingo	9,00 a 14,30 h
Museo de Bellas Artes	958 224843	Martes	14,30 a 20,00 h
		Miércoles a Sáb.	09,00 a 20,00 h
		Domingo	09,00 a 14,30 h
Casa Museo Manuel de Falla	958 229421	Martes a Sáb.	09,00 a 15,00 h
		Domingo, Lunes y festivos cerrado	
Museo de la Alhambra	958 226279	Martes a Sáb.	09,00 a 14,30 h
		Festivos cerrado	
Parque de las Ciencias	958 131900	Martes a Sáb.	10,00 a 19,00 h
		Domingo y festivos	10,00 a 15,00 h
		Cerrado del 15 al 30 de Septiembre.	